Walking the Story

Walking the Story

In the Steps of
Saints and Pilgrims

Jane Leach

British Library Cataloguing in Publication data
A catalogue record for this book is available
from the British Library

ISBN 978-1-905958-07-8

First published by Inspire
4 John Wesley Road
Werrington
Peterborough PE4 6ZP

Printed and bound in Great Britain by
Aldridge Print Group, Mitcham, Surrey

To Michael-Seán Paterson
who first introduced me to the Camino,

and to those many fellow pilgrims through the years
who have taught me
'What it means in daily living
to believe and to adore.'
[Fred Pratt-Green]

Acknowledgements

My thanks are due to a number of people who made the writing of this book possible: to the Wesley House Trustees who granted me the study leave both to walk and to write; to Philip and Sue Beuzeval, in whose house much of the text was drafted; to Janet Morley, and to my editor, Natalie Watson, whose wisdom and encouragement have guided this project; and to Oonagh O'Brien who has read countless drafts, made numerous suggestions, and supplied innumerable cups of coffee.

Jane Leach, June 2007

Contents

Introduction

Pilgrimage has been an image for the Christian life since biblical times – perhaps most famously developed by John Bunyan in *The Pilgrim's Progress*. Explored through hymns and liturgy, for many Christian people who have never been on a physical pilgrimage, the image is a rich one. Although pilgrimages were once central to the practice of Christian faith, since the Reformation they had waned in significance until the second half of the last century. Package holidays have opened up travel to the holy sites of Jerusalem and Rome, but the route across France and Spain to Santiago de Compostela has been revived as a pilgrimage which thousands of people each year now make on foot or by bicycle or on horseback.

This book tells the story of my pilgrimage from the French foothills of the Pyrenees, across the width of northern Spain to Santiago. Each chapter describes places and people and experiences associated with a stage of the journey, beginning as I set out from my home in Cambridge in Easter week of 2005 and ending in the holy city itself in time for Pentecost. For those interested in making the pilgrimage themselves there a map of the route marking places named in the text; contact details for the Confraternity of St James are included in the resources at the end of the book. The Confraternity issue pilgrim passports, sell English-language guides to the route and offer advice to pilgrims.

The book in outline

Chapter 1 begins in Cambridge and sets the scene, describing what it feels like to walk along an ancient pilgrim path. It explores the way in which a physical pilgrimage structures time and space and makes room for encounter with the God whose story of salvation is told in stone at church after church along the way. Throughout the chapter you are encouraged to consider the significant stories that shape your own life. How might you structure your life in order to be shaped more deeply by the Christian story?

Chapter 2 tells the story of my journey across the Pyrenees. It explores the significance to contemporary pilgrims of walking in the open air, exposed to the beauty and terror of creation and raises the question of how God relates to the creation. You are invited to take time to become aware of your own creatureliness through the rhythms of the natural world. How do you make time and space to encounter God in creation?

Chapter 3 describes the experience of walking through the red clay of the wine-growing region of La Rioja. It explores some of the images of Christ encountered on the way and particularly that of Christ, himself, as a pilgrim. The invitation of the chapter is to become more identified with the

God who identifies with us in Christ. What helps you to recognize your kinship with God in Christ and how do you help others to trust in this love which is at the heart of the universe?

Chapter 4 details the part of the journey in which I became most aware of the need for hospitality and companionship as I walked across the seemingly unending plains of Castille. It explores the role of Christians as guests of Christ at the feast of the heavenly banquet and suggests that those who would be hosts in the name of Christ need first to know how to be guests. The chapter encourages reflection on your own experiences of being a stranger. What do these experiences have to teach you about hospitality?

Chapter 5 is entitled 'Coming Home'. It describes the sensation of arriving in Santiago after five weeks of anticipation and explores this as a metaphor for coming home to the God who awaits us with open arms. Have you ever been anywhere that felt like a holy place? What role might such places play in nurturing the faith of those new to Christianity?

Reading this book

In the course of each chapter, you are invited to reflect upon key questions raised by the experience, and are encouraged, as I did, to keep a journal in which to note insights and issues to pursue. The questions in the margins are designed to help you interact with the text and make your own journey through the book. At the end of each chapter are six meditations. These are designed for personal use and if used daily after the reading of the chapter take a week to complete. Any reader using the book in this way will find that the whole book takes five weeks to read – a journey which mirrors the five weeks it took me to walk the route. Suggestions for further reading on the topics covered are made in the resources section at the end of the book.

Using this book as the basis for group discussion

At the end of the book there are suggestions for group work which relate to the five chapters. Any pilgrimage – whether literal or metaphorical – involves not only personal time for reflection and prayer, but companions with whom to share the journey. It is envisaged that house groups may use the book to stimulate conversation about the themes raised in the chapters or that discipleship groups may covenant to share their faith journeys as they read the book in tandem.

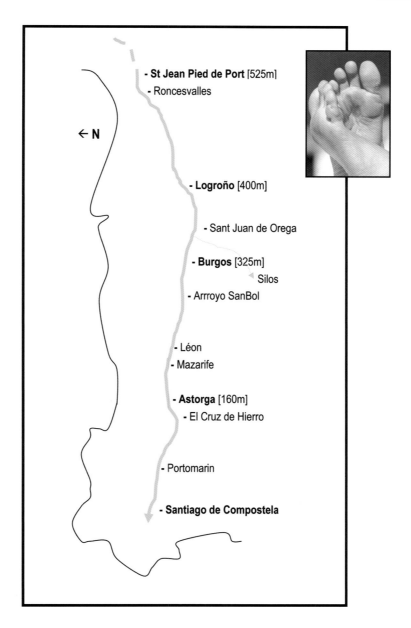

- **St Jean Pied de Port** [525m]
  - Roncesvalles

← N

- **Logroño** [400m]

- Sant Juan de Orega

- **Burgos** [325m]
  ◁ Silos
- Arrroyo SanBol

- Léon
- Mazarife

- **Astorga** [160m]
  - El Cruz de Hierro

- Portomarin

- **Santiago de Compostela**

A map of the pilgrim route from St Jean Pied de Port to Santiago de Compostela

1: Walking the Story
– setting out from home

*Yellow arrows mark the route the pilgrim must follow from
St Jean Pied de Port to Santiago. Photograph: Christine Polaček*

Setting out from home

Starting out on the road to Santiago felt like a huge freedom. I had said goodbye to family and colleagues and all the responsibilities of work and home. Used to a busy lifestyle in which I constantly juggle the competing concerns of work, home, community life, family and friends, suddenly there were few choices to be made: no need to prioritize, there was only walking to be done; no need to worry about what to wear, there was only what was clean; no need to work out the best route, all that was required was to look out for the yellow arrows and follow them.

From St Jean Pied de Port, high in the French Pyrenees, to Santiago de Compostela, some 500 miles to the west, the ancient pilgrimage route to the shrine of St James is marked with yellow arrows. Shining from trees and brick walls and from the stones of the road itself, through villages and city centres and across fields, the yellow markers funnel twenty-first-century pilgrims towards their destination. The boldness of the markers suggests, with the certainty of an ancient tradition that, despite all contemporary confusions, here is one clear way if we will accept the discipline of following it.

Setting out, pilgrims trust that their experience will be intensified and their perceptions will deepen as the road narrows towards its destination.

Once the pilgrim has walked through the pilgrim gate at St Jean Pied de Port the imagination stretches long and thin all the way to Santiago and although crossing the Pyrenees or walking across the plains of Castille the pilgrim is aware of space – of mountains and fields stretching as far as the eye can see – there is also a tangible sense of being on a narrow path. The hills and plains form a backdrop for the ancient snaking route that channels the pilgrim's mind towards the distant towers of Santiago's medieval cathedral of St James.

St Jean was the official starting place of my pilgrimage, but even as I left my home in Cambridge, catching the bus and then the plane from Stansted to Bilbao I did not feel like I was travelling to a holiday destination. Already clad in walking boots and strapped to my rucksack, the pilgrimage had begun. Unlike the medieval pilgrims who travelled to Santiago I had the option to fly part of the way. Most of them would have set out on foot to walk from their own homes through the lanes of England to the ports of Dover or Southampton. Having sailed across the Channel they would then have had to walk the length of France before reaching the Pyrenees. Yet even though I only walked from my front door to the bus station my heart was fixed on my destination. I was already on the road.

Setting out from home I was enjoying the freedom that perhaps my medieval predecessors had done. Released from the closed communities of small villages and the obligation to confess to their own parish priests – no one would have known them on the road! Yet I was anticipating too that the road would sometimes feel like hard work: when the sun was beating down there would be no respite; when the path started uphill; when the arrows were taking me through the industrial suburbs of a great city, the traffic roaring and the relentless concrete dual carriageways feeling soulless and endless, I imagined the temptation would be to get on a bus and take refuge in the romantic charm of a medieval city centre. And yet the ethos of the Camino is that the road is a discipline. Pilgrims practise the belief that even in the most unpromising of sections – through road works or when they feel least like getting out of bed in the morning – there is something of value to be learned in simply following the road. Pilgrims trust that their experience will be intensified and their perceptions will deepen as the road narrows towards its destination.

Even when the road feels barren, a pilgrim trusts that following it will yield a deeper kind of living than the wanderings of the tourist.

How are discipleship and discipline related in your experience?

The gospels describe the Christian way as the narrow way. At first glance this may confirm the view that Christianity is all about rules and prohibitions, yet Christians, like pilgrims, trust that sticking to the chosen path, even when it feels barren, will yield a deeper kind of living and a more profound way of loving and being loved, than the wanderings of the tourist who may choose the day's itinerary on a whim.

Experiencing this pilgrim route as it carried me across the breadth of northern Spain has led me to reflect more deeply about the way in which Christians use the word 'pilgrimage'. Accustomed to thinking of pilgrimage as an open-ended quest, I was struck instead by the discipline involved in a physical pilgrimage, and by the nature of Christian discipleship as discipline.

The narrow way

Arriving on that first evening in St Jean Pied de Port, the small French town which is the gateway to the Pyrenees, I explored the pilgrim gate which stands in the eastern wall of the town. As I walked through it, immediately the sensation was like being funnelled through a narrow gorge. I recalled an exhibit I had seen earlier in the day in the Guggenheim museum of contemporary art in Bilbao. On the ground floor of the museum there is a permanent exhibit through which it is possible to walk. Two 20-feet high sheets of bronze-coloured metal tower above the visitor, forming a tunnel that winds across the room. Once inside the tunnel, all that can be seen is the road. What is happening to the left or right, beyond the high walls, can only be dimly heard and imagined. What is real is the path, those walking ahead and behind, the beating of one's own heart and the anticipation of the light at the end of the tunnel.

Walking through the pilgrim gate reminded me of the museum exhibit because, once on the road, much of the rest of life fades. What is real is the path, those ahead and behind; those who have travelled this road before; one's own thoughts and feelings; and the anticipation of arriving in Santiago. Although there are no walls keeping the pilgrim to the straight and narrow, the yellow arrows, which I was beginning to identify snaking through the town, were constant reminders to my feet to keep to the path.

Also, like the experience of walking through the tunnel in the Guggenheim, walking the Camino means surrendering one's freedom, albeit for a short time. Once the path is chosen there is nothing to do but to follow it. Subsequent choices are few; concentration is centred upon this path and the sensations of walking along it: the confined space; the sound of footsteps and voices; the echoes. The pilgrim walks for a month or six weeks along a road which is prescribed. One may look up at the landscape to the north or south and wonder at the signposts on the main roads, pointing to other places, but the only places of significance are those on the route. These are the only places the guide books mention. These are the only places the pilgrim will see and they are the only places that, for the moment, matter. For only these places will bring the pilgrim closer to their destination at the end of the road.

The pilgrim surrenders their freedom trusting that following this one narrow road will be life-giving. It may be a sense of achievement in arriving that is anticipated; it may be the sights or people encountered along the way that the pilgrim imagines will be fruitful; but for many it is the journey inwards which comes to the fore. On this road, often, there is little to do but attend to the sensations of walking along it; to wonder at the experiences of others who walked this road in very different times; to listen to the resonances which bounce off the churches and standing crosses and monasteries which form the metaphorical walls of this road.

The invitation to the pilgrim is to listen to the echoes of their own heart.

The experience is most fruitful for those who can surrender themselves to it.
The invitation of the pilgrimage is to listen to the echoes of one's own heart.
Sometimes, this can be a lonely experience. When the mist closes in or the concrete desert of the industrial zone of a city stretches on and on, the challenge is to listen to one's own voice.

Few people find this an easy experience. Depending on our personalities we can spend much of our lives preoccupied with the voices of others, feeling swamped and silenced, trapped by others' impressions of us; or we can spend our lives talking in order to fill up the silences, drowning out the voices of others without listening even to what we, ourselves, are saying. But being confined to one road, there is opportunity to hear the echoes of one's own voice. This is not just because other distractions have been removed, but because the structure of the journey makes a contained space in which to examine difficult truths.

The holding ability of the route came home to me when I first suffered blisters. Compelled to walk in order to get to the next hostel, I found myself tapping into the pain of a bereavement I had carried for three years. Somehow, here, in this very structured environment I felt safe enough to let myself feel the emotions I had hardly dared to visit – the loss; the fury; the guilt. The structure of the day allowed time for introspection and time to get hold of these feelings; but it also imposed limits. I could not simply slide into depression and inaction as I might have done at home. I had to evacuate the hostel by 8 a.m.; I had to eat to keep the body going; there were other people to interact with; some needed my help. The route also imposed a timetable. It did not feel like entering a long dark tunnel with no end and I had the courage to enter the memories I needed to face because I knew it would not last forever. The route enabled me to pace myself. I did not have to do it all today. There would be tomorrow, but not all my tomorrows would be consumed.

A pilgrimage to a fixed destination has the ability to structure time and space to create a defined and potentially fruitful place in which to come to terms with oneself. T.S. Eliot comments that human beings cannot bear very much reality. Yet, we can, when held, bear a little at a time. In Christian understanding it is God who holds us. It is in God's embrace that we can dare, little by little, to face our own reality. Yet, holding of other kinds can lead us into the containing presence of God: the physical embrace of a friend is an obvious example, but even the routines of a structured day can release us from our surface concerns and offer the security we need in order to go deeper into the truth of who we are.

What 'disciplines' help you to listen to what your heart is saying?

Structure can sometimes feel like a negative thing. We can long to escape the dulling routines of our daily lives. The constraints of a timetable can make us feel restricted and confined. Yet structure not only limits experience, it also enables it. Perhaps this is most obvious in worship. The repetition of a short chorus or chant used as a structure can enable the worshipper to come close to God. Similarly, formal liturgy – like that of a Communion service – structures time. We know what is coming and so we can enter more deeply into prayer, allowing the skeleton of the service to carry us, familiar prayers becoming fleshed out as we reach beneath the surface of the words.

The Camino structures time and space in a way that enables the pilgrim to enter their own reality. Because life is paced out towards a destination, there is time and space in which to think and reflect and get beneath the surface of things. Yet, the destination is not neutral and the walls of the road do not merely bounce back the pilgrim's own thoughts. The destination of the pilgrim is, in some sense, the heavenly city, and the walls are formed by the history and iconography of the Christian story. These structure the pilgrim's experience in particular ways and suggest frameworks within which they might understand their own story. Already , as I set out from St Jean, my head was full of the landmarks, described by the pilgrim guides, that I would encounter: the Gate of Pilgrims, a place to leave behind what you do not need for your journey; Roncesvalles, a place in which to receive hospitality after the arduous journey across the Pyrenees; Arroyo Sanbol, a place to wash your feet and be cleansed; the Mount of Joy, a place in which to weep at the first sighting of your destination; so that by the time you arrive, you are ready, not just to stop walking, but to be welcomed into the life of heaven, represented in the joyful stones of the Portico de Gloria in the cathedral at Santiago.

The destination of the Christian pilgrim is, in some sense, the heavenly city.

The way of the cross

One of the most common symbols found on the Camino is that of the cross. The way is regularly punctuated by all kinds of crosses. Many commemorate pilgrims who have died on the road. My first assumption was that these pilgrims would have died long ago when the route was more dangerous and lonely to travel; when pilgrims had less effective clothing and were likely to be suffering from all kinds of diseases from which they were seeking healing. On closer inspection they turned out to be mostly quite recent: these were memorials to contemporary men and women who had died on the way of heart attacks or had been knocked down crossing main roads.

Such memorials are interspersed with medieval standing crosses. Originally they functioned as way markers and were part of the medieval route's attempt to assert itself against the conquered Muslim kingdoms. Often they depict Mary holding Jesus on one side and the crucifixion on the other. They are made of stone, and many are worn, but they attract attention because of their historical interest and because they reassure the pilgrim that they are on the right track. Some are placed high on surrounding hills and dominate the horizon for mile after mile. Some are placed in the centres of town squares and preside over marketplaces and traffic islands.

Crosses flank the Camino and their presence shapes the way.

Other crosses are found on the façades of churches. Many of these are part of friezes which tell the story of Jesus' life. Particularly common are the stories that surround Jesus' birth, carved into the capitals around the entrances to churches; also common are scenes including pilgrims: Jesus healing blind Bartimaeus who is dressed as a pilgrim; Jesus touching a leper, dressed as a pilgrim; a pilgrim standing at the foot of the cross.

Probably the most famous cross on the Camino Frances is the Cruz de Hierro, the high or iron cross. It stands near the highest point on the whole route, at 1500m and was said to have guided pilgrims across the plains towards the pass through the mountains of Léon. Its other function is to provide a place for pilgrims to leave something behind. The cross stands within a large cairn of stones and the tradition is to bring a stone from home. As one carries the stone mile after mile, the idea is to allow it to acquire the significance of that which one needs to let go of – guilt or anger; an addiction or habit; a relationship or group of friends. It is part of the preparation for entering the holy city and many people, of religious faith and none, find it a helpful stepping-stone along the way that focuses their thoughts, not on the surface of things, but on their direction in life.

What does the symbol of the cross mean to you?

Crosses flank the Camino and their presence shapes the Way. Layers of association seep into the mind – the death of other pilgrims; my own death; the possibility of dying on the way; the questions 'What is worth dying for?', 'What do I live for?' Encountering the cross of Jesus as a way marker prompts all kinds of questions: 'In what sense does the life and death of Jesus point the way for me? For others? What do my struggles have to do with the suffering of Christ? Was he raised from the dead? Is there resurrection for me?' Then, on finding pilgrims like me placed within the biblical stories, offered healing and restoration and purpose by the living Christ, further questions surface: 'Does Christ really have healing and belonging and direction for me? And if he does, what will be the cost?'

That these questions were raised for me, as a Christian, is hardly surprising, yet Christian faith as a way of life is difficult to avoid on the Camino. Through the images, churches and monasteries along the way, the Christian story presses itself on pilgrims of religious faith and none. It offers a way of interpreting life; it offers a pattern of living; it implies, at every turn, the way of the cross, through pain and betrayal and death to resurrection. It invites a conversation between the pilgrim's own story and the stories of other pilgrims and the Christian story told in stone.

Walking the story

The guidebooks to the Camino provide a great fund of stories for the imagination. Yet for the Christians who have walked this route for centuries, the way of the cross which this pilgrimage enacts – from entry through the narrow gate in St Jean to the vision of glory in Santiago – is not merely *a* story, but *the* prime story which makes sense of their lives and grants purpose and meaning. The Christian pilgrim is not merely walking the road, but walking the story of salvation.

Everyone loves a good story. Good stories are stories in which we can recognize ourselves and work ourselves out. Hence the popularity of film and soap opera, jokes and novels. Not only do human beings like stories, we need stories. We need a way of telling the story of our past. We need a way of imagining the story of our future. It is only by being able to place ourselves within a narrative that we have power to act: by understanding who we are, we know how to respond.

The story of salvation is God's vehicle for drawing human beings into the life of heaven.

Yet some of the narratives we inhabit are destructive for us. If, for example, we have spent our lives being told that we are hard and indifferent and the stories that illustrate this are told again and again, it is difficult not to believe it and enact this 'truth' in the future. Lots of time and money is paid to therapists trying to construct a different narrative for ourselves in which we may play a different part. Often, however, it is not just that we need a different part in the story, we need a different overarching story. Embedded in the story that I am hard and indifferent is a view of human personality that is fixed and unchanging. Therapy works on a different assumption. To engage in counselling means participating in a story with an open ending. In the overarching story which therapy tells, change is possible.

These insights into the shaping nature of story have prompted theologians to approach Christian doctrine as story. This is not simply suggesting that the Bible or Christian history are full of good stories, not even stories with morals. Rather, this approach suggests that the story of salvation which Christians tell which begins in creation and ends in the re-creation of all that is through the person and work of Jesus Christ is God's vehicle for drawing us into the life of heaven.

What first drew you into God's story of salvation?

Pilgrimage is an invitation into the Christian story. It is an invitation to trust in the overarching storylines of God's love and care for everything God has made; of God's longing for intimacy with all God's people; of God's presence in the life and death and resurrection of Jesus Christ as God's prime way of drawing people to Godself. These articles of faith, though, are not primarily intellectual propositions to be accepted or rejected, they are the bones of a story, the flesh of which needs to be our own lives. Accepting an invitation into the Christian story is to find our true identity as a creature whom God has made; as a person made for intimacy with God; as someone for whom Christ died. We begin to understand our stories as part of one great story, told throughout the ages, of love and longing and fulfilment in Christ.

Finding ourselves in the story

For this to happen, what is required is that we surrender to the story. In terms of a pilgrimage, this means not only surrendering to the experience of walking one path; it means opening ourselves to the story told by the route itself. Already I had a sense of this as I wandered the streets of St Jean in anticipation of beginning in earnest in the morning. But it was some two weeks later that I had an experience of being woven into the story of salvation.

Inside the monastery of San Juan de Ortega some 160 miles from St Jean there is a famous eleventh-century depiction of the nativity [see page 24]. It is a beautiful and striking sculpture and it is unique in that the capital on which it is carved is placed in the church so that it is illuminated by a brilliant shaft of light only at the equinoxes. My first thought was to photograph it, arrogantly assuming that I could do a better job than that in the magazine I had read. What I did not realize was that the lighting in that picture was not the flash I was using but the sun at the equinox. Someone with greater patience than I had sat and waited in the dark for the light to catch the annunciation.

In any event, my ambitions were thwarted. The battery on my camera, upset by the cold and the altitude of the mountain range we had just crossed, meant I was powerless to take any pictures. Cursing about having come all this way, it then occurred to me that I could sketch the figures. For me, maybe this was the equivalent of waiting in the dark for the sun to be in position. I sat for an hour, looking in detail at the lines of the faces and fall of the clothing and the sensitivity of the hands – the midwife holding Mary as she slept after the birth; the angel's head on Joseph's head, one hand on the baby's feet and the other resting on Joseph, communicating to him her concern;

the gifts of the magi, hanging above the cradle; the intimacy of the ox and the ass, almost licking the baby Jesus in their curiosity, in the praise of their presence.

The point is not the quality of the representation I produced. The point is the time I spent entering into the spirit of the carving, seeking to understand its import; wondering about those who made it; marvelling at the raw humanity of the figures. I was moved beyond words to see Mary being treated as a human mother who has given birth, not kneeling over the cradle as an icon of female spirituality, but exhausted, asleep and held.

I began with attention to the detail of the image and was led into meditating on its significance. Finally, through my absorption in the image, I was drawn into the story behind it, and then I began to discern a question addressed to me by the same God who addressed Mary in the annunciation and Joseph in his dreams, 'Are you willing to become?'

The postmodern story

For many people such an approach to story is both deeply attractive and deeply difficult. In our time human beings are just as fascinated with stories as people have ever been. Many long for the meaning and rootedness which our ancestors seemed to find so easily within a religious tradition but are suspicious of any story which claims to have universal meaning. For many contemporary people stories are to be collected and critiqued rather than being allowed to define who we are.

What gives you a sense of meaning and rootedness in your life?

Part of the problem is that in the postmodern version of reality all the great religions, all the great philosophies, are reduced to being *mere* stories. Any story which claims to have universal significance is held to be the product of one human group which seeks power over other groups by trivializing or suppressing the stories of those who do not fit the metanarrative. So postmodern people tend to be eclectic, treating religious traditions and secular philosophies as pots of wisdom to be dipped into. The very idea of choosing to follow any one path seems counterintuitive, if not absurd.

Many contemporary people are looking for wisdom by which to live.

The approach to life which resists being drawn into any grand story and prefers instead to be the author of its own was presented to me forcefully by a young man I met on the road. We first met outside a wayside hermitage where there were discarded palms on the path from the Palm Sunday worship. As I sat, idly seeing whether I could remember how to make a palm cross we began a series of conversations about life and faith that lasted all the way to Santiago. David was clearly searching for something. As his story unfolded it became apparent that his upbringing had left him with a lot to contend with. He had spent long periods of his adult life doing nothing but working in a bar and getting stoned. His father had disappeared from his life when he was a child; he did not have friends and confessed that he probably would not keep up with anyone he had met on the Camino, though he was one of the most thoughtful and hospitable people I met. He wanted to be his best self; he wanted to live well; he wanted to believe in himself; he wanted to write a novel. He was looking for some wisdom that would help him.

He had a book of Paulo Coelho's with him which offers a thought for each day culled from an eclectic mix of Catholic teaching and Arthurian legend; he spoke about his mother who had become interested in Buddhism and had found it very helpful. He wanted to go to India to explore Buddhist teaching; at the same time he said he believed in God and Jesus and several times asked about the possibility of baptism.

What is the deep wisdom out of which you live your life?

To me, being a Buddhist and being baptized as a Christian are mutually exclusive. Being Christian is not simply about believing in God. It is about understanding the world and oneself from the point of view of the Christian story. One might find in other religious traditions echoes of this story; one might be open to one's understanding of the Christian story being challenged by the insights of another tradition, but to be Christian means affording ultimate authority to the story of Jesus Christ.

For David, placing himself within the Christian story in this way represented an unacceptable loss of freedom. He wanted to be free to be himself; to make his own way; to discover wisdom where he could find it; to follow one path felt restrictive and oppressive – too full of rules and regulations for him to be himself.

There are some good things about this critical attitude towards totalizing narratives. An uncritical acceptance of a version of reality devised by others to suit their interests without regard for the interests of others is oppressive. An emphasis, for example, upon obedience in marriage has masked much domestic violence against women. Encouraging women to listen to their own voices is an important corrective in a society that has ignored and marginalized the experience, wisdom and priorities of women in the past.

Yet the postmodern ethos suggests, not just that *oppressive* grand narratives are to be resisted, but that all grand narratives are suspect. Remaining free from being tied to any particular path – being a free spirit – is seen as a virtue. Partly this may be making a virtue out of necessity. It is no longer possible, for example, for most people to remain working for the same firm all of their lives. It is rarer for people to live in the same town all their lives, let alone in the same house, and even if a person remains, the community they once knew is likely to have changed beyond recognition. Most people no longer grow up within a particular religious tradition but are aware of many. A certain degree of flexibility is necessary to postmodern people in order to survive in the contemporary western world.

In such a climate, work, place, family and religious traditions have become pots to dip into. To imagine living and working in one place; attending the same chapel for years; being married to the same person for years, for many people feels impossibly restrictive and narrow. Yet at the same time there is nostalgia for a way of life and a sense of rootedness that has been lost.

For Zygmunt Bauman, who has written extensively on postmodernity, the typical self in western society today is a vagabond which he defines as

> a pilgrim without a destination; a nomad without an itinerary ... the vagabond wanders through unstructured space; like a wanderer in the desert who only knows of such trails as are marked with his own footprints and blown off again by the wind the moment he passes, the vagabond structures the site he happens to occupy at the moment, only to dismantle the structure again as he leaves. Each successive spacing is local and temporary – episodic.[1]

There was a growing awareness as we walked that freedom comes from commitment to a path that is not of one's own making.

Reading this it could be argued that the recent trend towards going on pilgrimage might be a reflection of the dis-ease in western society. It might be understood as escapism from the demands of commitment to work and place and relationships. But although the lives of some of the pilgrims I encountered evidenced precisely this kind of homelessness – successions of jobs, homes, relationships and a sense of mystification about why anyone would choose to follow a particular religious tradition – there was also a growing awareness as we walked, among some, of the freedom that comes from commitment to a path that is not of one's own making.

Whom do you trust to shape your life?

For Christians, however, freedom comes, not merely from the security of following any known path. Even the most destructive of suicide cults will offer that. For Christians it is crucial that the stories that we allow ourselves to inhabit reflect the truth at the heart of the universe. It matters which stories we inhabit, because these will have power over us. To recognize ourselves in a story is to allow ourselves to be named by the author of the story. Partly this is an acknowledgement of the truism that as human beings we are not the sole authors of our own stories: we come to be who we are through the naming of us that others do. But it is also the making of a choice that it is the God we see in Jesus Christ, and no other, whom we trust to name us. It is God in Christ who is telling the story about us that we recognize to be most profoundly true.

The way of freedom

To become Christian is to recognize ourselves in the story that God is telling. This involves a surrender of the illusory freedom that we are the sole authors of our own stories and a recognition that genuine freedom comes from being fully known and loved. To be a pilgrim is to enter into the story God is telling and to allow ourselves to be written more deeply into the narrative.

For Paul, freedom is the condition in which Christians live. Christians, through their relationship with Christ, have been set free from fear, from the need to justify themselves, from sin, from death. In fact Christ sets us free from all that keeps us from God's loving presence. To many contemporary ears this might seem an odd basis for freedom. Freedom is usually understood to be based in choice. For Paul, freedom is based in the love of God. This is the only solid basis for freedom, for it is the only kind of freedom which is based in the truth of who we are: children of God.

Freedom for Paul is not the freedom to be who we like, but the freedom to become who we are.

When Paul speaks about the freedom of the children of God, it is the freedom that comes from knowing we are loved; from knowing we belong; from knowing that we have a real identity rooted and grounded in the love at the heart of the universe. This is not the freedom to be who we like. It is the freedom to be who we are. It is not the freedom that comes from independence, a freedom that so often leaves us isolated, homeless and restless. It is the freedom that comes from radical dependence.

The contrast between the kind of freedom that is based on wanting to be independent and the kind which is based on our radical dependence upon God is painted sharply in Jesus' parable of the prodigal son (Luke 15). The younger son is free to leave home and he does so. He takes his half of the inheritance and spends it on what he thinks will set him free. He does what he likes. He is a law unto himself. He spends it on all the things that money can buy, and while the money lasts he has the illusion of being in control. He is desperate to be independent of his father, to find his own way; to be his own person, and so the father lets him go. Yet all the while the son is away the father grieves.

The father grieves, not just because he misses his son and wants to see him, but because he knows the son's attempt to find freedom is doomed to failure. It is doomed because it is not based on the truth of who the son is. All the son's efforts to be free are in fact defences against the truth that his very being cries out for the love of his father.

Real freedom comes from allowing ourselves to be loved by the one who knows us and longs for us to be at home in ourselves.

The story is a parable. It is not primarily about the relationship between human fathers and sons. It is about the truth that real freedom is allowing ourselves to be loved by the one who knows us and longs for us to be at home in ourselves. This cannot be done by pretending we have no real home or that we can make our home anywhere we like. In fact, the only place we will be truly happy and truly ourselves is in the knowledge that we are completely known and completely loved. Such love can be embodied for us in those who truly love us and want the best for us, yet all such love has its source in God's very self.

This is the story which any Christian pilgrimage enacts. Christian pilgrims commit themselves to one path in the belief that this is the path of freedom. It is the path to the knowledge that we truly are ourselves when we allow ourselves to be held as children of God.

16

Such freedom does not come cheaply. We fear the love that knows us because, to receive it, we have to come to know ourselves too. This is a painful process and often we would prefer the cheaper routes to freedom that are offered in the stories our society enacts: the escapism of drugs or alcohol; the freedom from facing the age we actually are as promised by creams and dyes and plastic surgery; the freedom that money can buy to do whatever we want. For this reason, Christians need help to keep themselves attentive to the story which God is telling. Believing that true freedom comes from God alone is one thing, continually entering through the narrow gate of discipleship is another.

How can Christians help one another to be attentive to the love story God is telling?

Because we are constantly influenced by competing grand stories of what it is to be human, what will make us happy, what will set us free, we need structures of life that will help us to enter time and again into the values of the kingdom of God. It is salutary to think about how much time we spend listening to the drip, drip, drip of our image-driven culture, receiving messages about the way our hair, clothes and homes should look; by comparison, how much time do we spend allowing the images and stories of the Christian tradition to shape us? If we are convinced it is the way of Christ that will set us free, we need to keep putting ourselves in the place where we allow the narratives of the Christian tradition to have imaginative power over our lives.

A Christian pilgrimage is one way of engaging in the Christian tradition which enables us to find ourselves written into the story of salvation. It happens as we commit ourselves to one path and discover the safe place that a structured path can offer for entering beneath the surface of ourselves. It happens as we find our stories woven together with the stories of pilgrims throughout the ages and are drawn into conversation with the faith that sustained them. It happens as we open ourselves to what God is saying to us through the stories told in ancient stones.

As I explored St Jean and perused the guidebooks I could feel this process already beginning. I was looking forward to this pilgrimage as a way of allowing myself to be more profoundly shaped by the Christianity story. Yet devoting time and space for prayer and meditation is possible anywhere, and so is spending time entering into a story from the Bible and allowing it to speak into our lives. Bible notes, prayer handbooks and praying with others can discipline our prayers; many churches and even museums contain religious images with which we may sit, allowing them to resonate with our experience.

Pilgrimage is a challenge to Christians to develop disciplines of life that will help us tap into the transformative power of God's saving love.

In this way, the image of pilgrimage becomes a broad invitation to us to develop disciplines of life that will enable us to inhabit the Christian story and draw on its transformative power, allowing the God who knows us to love us; allowing this love to set us free.

17

Day 1
Enter through the narrow gate

*Enter through the
narrow gate... for the
gate is narrow and the
road is hard that
leads to life, and there
are few who find it.*

Matthew 7.13–14

St Jean Pied de Port is the gateway to the Pyrenees and the gateway to the Camino Frances. Passing through the Gate of Pilgrims, pictured here, implies submitting to the disciplines of pilgrimage: pilgrims must leave home behind and carry only a few possessions; they must walk all the way on their own feet, carry their own pack, sleep in the designated hostels, and submit their pilgrim passport for inspection at the end of the road.

In every generation those who would be disciples of Jesus must leave things behind, dedicate time to spend in his company and accept that they will be changed. The reward will be life in all its fullness, but Jesus is clear from the outset – this is no easy road.

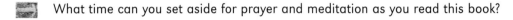 What time can you set aside for prayer and meditation as you read this book?

 What occupations or goals will you set aside in order to make the time?

To be a pilgrim involves a personal choice to make a journey, and yet all pilgrims find themselves in the company of others who share the way. In the same way, to be a disciple involves a personal calling, yet each disciple is called into the company of the faithful, to journey with others.

With whom will you share your thoughts and questions so that they can companion you on the road?

Lord Jesus Christ,
you called your first disciples to follow you,
and they left their father and their nets in the boat and went after you.
Whether we are called to set out in faith
or to practise a deeper faithfulness at home,
give us grace to leave behind what we do not need,
courage to persevere when the way is tough and unrewarding,
and find us faithful companions along the way.
Amen.

Day 2
Rooted and grounded in love

I pray that, according to the riches of his glory, he may grant that you may be strengthened in your inner being with power through his Spirit, and that Christ may dwell in your hearts through faith, as you are being rooted and grounded in love.

Ephesians 3.16–17

In the monastery at Samos, one of the brothers lights the Easter Candle as the community gathers to celebrate the Feast of the Ascension.

Pilgrimage is an example of a spiritual discipline which operates as a means of grace. It is through structured activities such as prayer, the reading of Scripture and the sharing of Holy Communion, that human beings become more deeply rooted and grounded in the love of God. The life of the Christian is not only shaped by moments of great wonder and insight but, routinely, by the books we read and the songs we sing and the time we make to become alive to God's presence.

  Think about the ways you usually pray. Might a chanted prayer or chorus help to create a space for a deep encounter with God?

  Try repeating the ancient Jesus prayer: 'Lord Jesus Christ, have mercy on me, a sinner.' As you repeat the words allow your breathing to slow and your attention to focus on Christ.

The use of physical space can likewise help worshippers to approach God. Approaching the Communion table is an example of a physical movement mirroring an internal attitude. The time it takes to walk the length of the aisle helps the worshipper to be ready to receive. Similarly, the whole outline of the Communion service paces the time towards the moment of receiving, making space on the way for adoration, confession, forgiveness, hearing God's word, praying for the world and making peace with one's neighbour.

  Think about where you normally pray. Might walking a regular route help structure time with God?

  How helpful do you find structured worship with regular points for particular prayers? Try using a formal order for morning or evening prayer for a month and reflecting on that experience.

Day 3
Our true selves

If any want to become my followers, let themselves and take up their cross and follow me. For those who want to save their life will love it, and those who lose their life for my sake and for the sake of the gospel, will save it. For what will it profit them to gain the whole world and forfeit their life? Indeed, what can they give in return for their life?

Mark 8.34b–37

This photograph captures part of the Cruz de Hierro - or high cross - that dominates the pass through the mountains of Léon. Here pilgrims leave behind the stones they have carried from home and symbols of their hard-won struggles to discover their true selves.

The Christian life is often described in terms of self denial. Although sacrifices will be asked of us, God never asks us to give up being ourselves, rather to become more profoundly the people we were created to be. Often it is easier to keep our deepest selves hidden fearful that our naked selves will be rejected and so we clothe ourselves in all kinds of masks to prevent our true selves being discovered and damaged by others. We indulge in fantasies about our own independence and invulnerability, surrounding ourselves with possessions and other marks of success, drowning out the inner voice that dare not be loved. Jesus warns that following our instincts for comfort and self-protection will mean we lose touch with our true selves. It is in giving up these instincts and risking being known that we shall discover who we really are.

 Are you someone who speaks often but rarely pauses to listen to your own heart?

 Is your head so full of what others are saying that you struggle to hear your own voice?

 What prevents you from hearing your own inner voice?

 What is this voice saying?

Jesus does not ask us to leave our struggles to be ourselves behind. Rather, we are to bring these struggles with us on our journey of faith. This is our cross. What Jesus promises is that as we allow ourselves to be held by the love of God which spends itself for us on the cross, so we shall find ourselves more able to listen to our own inner voice, more able to risk knowing ourselves as we are and more able to spend ourselves in his service.

Loving God,
we struggle to be ourselves:
we hide in disguises of our own making;
we grab at the masks the world offers to us;
we rejoice in the things we own and the respect we have earned.
Teach us to listen to the voice within
that longs to be met and loved for itself alone.
Give us courage to begin our pilgrimage
from where we really are,
and to accept no cheap substitutes
for your costly love revealed on the cross.
Amen.

Day 4
Will you become?

In the sixth month the angel Gabriel was sent by God to a town in Galilee called Nazareth, to a virgin engaged to a man whose name was Joseph, of the house of David ...

Luke 1.26

In this eleventh-century frieze from San Juan de Ortega, Mary at first raises her hands in amazement [far left] before recognizing the thread of God's story of salvation in the words of Gabriel and embracing her part in the unfolding drama.

Joseph becomes woven into the story of God's salvation through his dreams. In this depiction the angel communicates with him by laying her head upon his and touching the sleeping child in a gesture of protection.

Mary and Joseph were both called by God into an unknown future. They said yes to a journey of faith without knowing quite where it would lead and what it would entail. They allowed God to become the author of their story, accepting as they travelled on that journey, to Bethlehem, to Egypt and finally, with Jesus, to Jerusalem, that they themselves would be transformed.

In what ways do you hope to be changed as you make the journey of faith?

Are there things you fear might need to change?

Mary and Joseph had plans for their lives. They were betrothed to be married. They had a place in their home community of Nazareth. They were not expecting their lives to be dramatically caught up into the drama of God's salvation.

Following the Christian way opens disciples to the risk of having the plans for their lives transformed.

Will you come and follow me if I but call your name?
Will you go where you don't know and never be the same?[2]

All human beings have unspoken expectations about the ways their lives will work out: expectations about whether they will marry or not; about working patterns; even about the age at which they expect to die. Often we are not aware of these 'scripts' for our lives until they are challenged.

Looking back, in what ways has your life worked out as you expected?

Where can you discern God at work?

Creator God,
weaving your story of purpose and promise
through lives that say yes,
when the track we are on comes to an end
and the direction our lives are taking no longer makes sense,
give us faith to trust that we are still written on the palm of your hand.
Amen.

Day 5

The glorious freedom of the children of God

Charles Mackesy, 'Prodigal
daughter'

But when he came to himself he said, 'How many of my father's hired hands have bread enough and to spare, but here I am dying of hunger! I will get up and go to my father and I will say to him, "Father, I have sinned against heaven and before you; I am no longer worthy to be called your son; treat me like one of your hired hands."' So he set off and went to his father. But while he was still far off, his father saw him and was filled with compassion; he ran and put his arms around him and kissed him.

Luke 15.17–20

The story of the prodigal son has all kinds of associations but at its heart is a son who thinks that freedom can be found in getting away and doing what he likes. He spends all that his father has given him on all the freedoms that money can buy, but in the end these are empty freedoms because they are not based on the truth of who he is, a beloved child of his father. This is the last thing he wants to be. Yet the son did not leave home because he was free; he was driven away by his inability to bear the bonds of love, by his fear of being known. When the paths of his choosing have proved to be dead ends, the son gives up all hope of freedom. He chooses slavery back at home, where, in spite of himself, he knows he will be well treated. The way home is hard. The son must face the truth of himself and the selfishness and waste of what he thought would set him free. Yet though the path home is hard, astonishingly, it turns out to be the way of freedom. The love that meets him is all that his heart ever desired, welcoming him, not as a slave, but as the beloved son and heir.

Pilgrimage has always presented pilgrims with a choice. It can be a form of escape – an opportunity to run away from the things about ourselves and our lives that we find difficult – or it can be a way of coming to our senses and returning home to the God who loves us for ourselves.

 Are you in the process of running from the presence of God, or of returning home?

 How can you tell?

As human beings we oscillate between fear and love. We fear we are not lovable. We run from the love that would prove us wrong. God is patient. Though our running grieves him, nothing can diminish his delight when we dare to trust and freely come home.

Gracious God,
when we think that running is freedom,
bring us to our senses.
When we fill our lives with freedoms that leave us empty,
make us yearn for your presence.
When we are ready to come home,
hold us in our shame
until we are filled with all the fullness of your love.
Amen.

Day 6
Go, sell all you have

The kingdom of heaven is like treasure hidden in a field,
which someone found and hid; then in his joy he goes
and sells all he has and buys that field.

Matthew 13.44–45

Human beings long to be free. We often imagine that choice is at the heart of freedom. But there is little freedom in endless options. There is little freedom in the fragmented heart that goes in many directions at once. A far deeper freedom comes from giving yourself wholeheartedly. What matters is finding the pearl of great price that is worth committing all that we have to possessing and following the path that will take us back to the field in which we glimpsed it.

When Paul speaks about the freedom of the children of God, it is the freedom that comes from knowing we are loved, from knowing we belong, from knowing that we have a real identity rooted and grounded in the love at the heart of the universe. This is the pearl of great price. Many people have fleeting glimpses of such a sense of joy and wholeness. The path of discipleship places God's love for us and the whole of creation at the heart of life. Nothing is more valuable. Nothing can make us more whole. Wholeness comes in giving the gift of our whole selves.

 Think of an occasion when you have been able to give yourself wholeheartedly to someone or something.

 What does this experience have to say about wholeness?

The following is a prayer from the Methodist Covenant Service. It suggests that wholeness is found in giving ourselves wholeheartedly to the God who gives himself wholeheartedly to humankind in Jesus Christ. The life of Christian discipleship is a journey into this prayer.

I am no longer my own but yours,
Your will, not mine, be done in all things,
Wherever you may place me,
In all that I do and in all that I may endure;
When there is work for me and when there is none;
When I am troubled and when I am at peace.
Your will be done when I am valued
And when I am disregarded;
When I find fulfilment and when it is lacking;
When I have all things, and when I have nothing.
I willingly offer all I have and am to serve you
    as and where you choose.
And now, glorious and blessed God,
You are mine and I am yours. So be it.
And the covenant now made on earth,
Let it be ratified in heaven.[3]
Amen.

29

2: Pilgrim through this Barren Land
– over the Pyrenees from St Jean to Logroño

The wind whips through the pass at Alto San Roque
as mist engulfs the path

Over the Pyrenees from St Jean to Logroño

I awoke in the hostel in St Jean to the sound of pilgrims rustling plastic bags. They were dressing and packing their rucksacks in the dark, putting everything back in its waterproof packaging ready for the journey. Disturbing the cat which had crept onto my bunk, I got up and began to do the same, feeling nervous. Today I was to cross the Pyrenees. After a breakfast of bread and cheese in the tiny kitchen, a small group of us set off with our walking sticks clicking on the cobbled street and went out of the town through the western gate, the figure of Christ the Good Shepherd urging us on with his raised staff.

Ahead, a thin trickle of pilgrims was heading off bravely into the sunshine. Within yards we too were walking uphill, the foothills of the Pyrenees rising up before us. The early morning air was tinged with ice, but the steaming sun soon burnt away the rising mist to reveal extraordinary views of distant snowy peaks and delicate spring flowers. It felt good to be alive and to feel the cold air in the bottom of my lungs as I peeled off layers of clothing.

As the weather was so good, most of us chose the higher path – the route Napoleon had taken, already well-worn by pilgrims 200 years ago. This path is often closed because of snow and high winds in the winter; even so, every year pilgrims lose their lives on this road. But today the snow was melting and spring flowers were appearing and the verges were rustling with lizards and toads. On the lower slopes horses stamped and snorted and as we climbed higher wild cattle could be glimpsed in the distance. Everyone seemed to be enjoying the spring weather. As the path became steeper, the views only became more spectacular, and I felt like the medieval pilgrim who commented that he had climbed so high he could not fail to see God.

When I'd set out from home my mind had already been fixed on Santiago. I had read the guidebooks and walked the route in my imagination. In my head it was marked by crosses and monasteries and yellow arrows. I knew there were mountains. I had expected them to present a challenge and an obstacle, but I had not anticipated my attention being drawn so dramatically to the beauty of the physical landscape. Yet listening to my own heart and talking with fellow pilgrims it became clear that for contemporary people part of the delight of the experience is spending five weeks in the open air.

For some, this is not an explicitly religious activity at all: their focus is upon health and fitness and enjoyment of the natural world, the medieval route is simply a well-worn path through beautiful countryside. For others, who may have no formal faith, the chance to return to more natural rhythms and to spend time in the natural world is a spiritual matter. For me the experience of being outside for five weeks highlighted the ways in which my usual lifestyle dulls my awareness. Here I experienced the

Pilgrimage is one way to enter into the natural world as an arena in which God might be encountered.

natural world and my own physicality as precious parts of God's creation, and as arenas of holiness in which God might be encountered.

Even on this first day it was becoming clear that the pilgrimage to Santiago is a physical journey through a physical landscape of beauty and barrenness. The landscape and the weather shape the days. Horizons are dominated by breathtaking views which lift the spirits and raise the heart in thanksgiving to God; then the scene changes and the mountains are shrouded in mist and gloom. With nowhere to go but onwards, however you feel, whatever the weather or the terrain, the experience of walking on one's own feet, at the mercy of the elements, is a vivid reminder that human beings, albeit sophisticated, are vulnerable creatures too.

Human vulnerability and dependence upon God are prominent themes in the Bible. Genesis records that human beings are creatures, made of the dust of the earth and part of the ecology of God's creation. Recent global history, however, has taken people away from a symbiotic relationship with the land towards models of exploitation which have left the land exhausted and many of its indigenous peoples dispossessed. Closer to home the craving for cottages in the country and retreats to deserted spots bear witness to our awareness of our estrangement from the rhythms of the seasons and from the art of listening to the needs of our own bodies for rest and simple foods.

In an age when serious questions must be faced about the relationship between human activity and the health of the planet, a renewed attention to our own creatureliness and the natural world as the arena of God's self-disclosure might help the human race to develop a healthier pattern of living for ourselves, our fellow creatures and for the earth itself. Taking seriously the physical dimension of pilgrimage is one way to enter into the natural world as the arena of God's healing presence and to be drawn into God's restoration of the whole creation.

Taking the time

One of the reasons why the physical journey across a physical landscape is such a striking feature of a contemporary pilgrimage is because we, unlike our medieval predecessors, are not used to travelling on foot. At walking pace the landscape changes slowly. After several hours of walking on that first day we could still see St Jean, gradually contracting to the size of a model village in the distance. Conceding that this was only the first day and the climb was steep, we allowed ourselves to take time, pausing to eat lunch and to take a siesta, watching the vultures circling overhead as they tried to decide whether or not we were still moving.

Do you feel that life is too fast? What helps you to slow down?

It need not take a pilgrimage to slow life down to walking pace. Yet, used to rushing from one place to another, by plane if necessary, time seems to many of us to be an elastic commodity into which we can cram more by speeding up. For some of us, perhaps, it takes walking for days on end to convince us that time cannot be hurried. Walking pace is always walking pace and although we cover less ground, perhaps we receive more.

One of the most important things that happened to me on the Camino was the loss of my watch. I had chained it and my travel torch to the frame of the bunk-bed so I could indulge my obsession of needing to know what time it is when I wake in the night. Having walked several miles the following morning before I realized it was missing, it was then too late to turn back and I was stuck without the means to tell the time. I began to realize how much of my time I spend racing against the clock and how this behaviour pervades even my sleeping hours. After my initial anxiety, I began to enjoy the sensation of only having a vague idea of the time. I would hear a distant clock strike the half-hour with no idea whether this was 4.30, 5.30 or 6.30, and with nothing to rush on to I could experience the unaccustomed freedom of needing to do nothing other than sit and watch the black kites circling overhead, or watch the storks stalking up and down some parapet or listen to the frogs chirruping in the stream.

In the contemporary western world few people can afford to live without diaries and clocks. In the service of the global market, our lives are dominated by the demands of work. We work long hours both to produce and to consume and we must be prepared to be flexible: to move house, to retrain, to change jobs. Novelty is valued; busyness is endemic (especially in the Church); in many households it is difficult to find time even to eat together. The structure of the global market means that working hours are often not within our control, and yet even in our leisure time we are often rushing anxiously about trying to cram in as much as possible, forgetting that relationships take time to grow and develop; that bodies and minds need time to rest; that silence and stillness are needed for healing.

In western culture it is easy to forget that relationships take time; that bodies and minds need time; that silence and stillness are needed for healing.

Jesus makes the point by asking the disciples to think about wild lilies: 'Consider the lilies, how they grow: they neither toil nor spin; yet I tell you, even Solomon in all his glory was not clothed like one of these' (Luke 12.27). Jesus uses the example to suggest to his disciples that they slow down; that they remember the universe will continue to be held in being without their efforts; that they meditate upon natural things to recover a sense of proportion and dispel their anxiety. This is the wisdom of the Jewish Sabbath. The people of Israel are commanded to stop work and remember that the world does not depend upon them but is held in being by God's sustaining grace.

Understanding ourselves as pilgrims on an earth which is held in being by God's intimate and intricate care gives us permission to slow down and resist the claims of the 24/7 society. It also gives us space to remember that human beings, like the rest of creation, are made for God's delight, and not simply for work. Moreover, made in the image of God, human beings are called to share in God's delight over the whole creation.

Delight also takes time. It requires that we become present to the here and now; that we allow plants and creatures and the physical stuff of the world to have their own existence and integrity independent of our use for them. Delight requires that we take the time to see each leaf or wing in its particularity; to savour smell and taste and colour; to rejoice that things are as they are. To delight in this way is to be drawn into God's perspective and to recover something of the image of God in us.

Delight is an important corrective to the possessive attitudes that characterize contemporary western culture. The philosopher Martin Heidegger identified the attitude of possessiveness as central to the problems of western culture. He complained that when faced with natural objects we see them as things to be categorized and catalogued so we can fit them into our schemes of understanding the world. We want to know their properties and potential so we can put them to use in our machines and medicines. We try to capture them in concepts that put us in control as those who label other creatures and the material world as objects at our disposal. On the scale of the multinational company the natural world is reduced to materials for the next project and indigenous peoples are reduced to cheap labour; on the scale of the individual's leisure time, the desire to seize and possess is illustrated by the desire to photograph.

Think about the holidays and day trips you take. How able are you to be present to what you see and experience?

The temptation for all of us who own cameras is to treat physical places as fodder for the photo album. We leap out of the car, frame a shot and leap back in, consuming the product we have made in the privacy of our living-rooms. Even taking photographs to show others can be an evasion of the possibility of being touched by what we see.

Having taken 600 stills on this one journey across northern Spain this is not a criticism levelled at others rather than myself and I evidently still believe that photographs have their uses. However, it is easy and all too tempting to observe the experience rather than to be immersed in it. The camera lens can get in the way of a direct relationship between ourselves and what is going on. Not only does the camera require us to be selective in framing what we see – choosing a view often before our perspective has had a chance to be changed by what is happening around us – but photography can be a way of seeking to possess what we cannot take home. Moreover, digital photography now gives us the facility to improve what we see – we can mould the environment to fit our aesthetic ideas electronically even if we cannot change it physically.

Taking a decision to make life a pilgrimage involves putting aside the functional attitudes that normally shape our approach to the material world and becoming alert to the physical environment on its own terms. We become aware of the shapes and colours and the sounds and smells of the world. We begin to listen to something other than our own desire to shape and mould the world, and instead start to move in tune with the rhythms of our bodies and our fellow creatures. We begin to open ourselves to animals and plants and physical objects as genuinely other objects with their own existence. Through attentiveness to them in their particularity, we not only join in the delight which God takes in the world he has made, but we enter into the pain of the earth and its people and the groaning of all creation as it waits for fulfilment. We take time, not only to rejoice in the goodness of creation, but to lament over its pollution, over climate change, over the accelerating rate at which species are becoming extinct. In doing so, we are drawn further into the perspective of the God who is weaving together all things for good with those who love him.

Remembering our own creatureliness

On that first day as I climbed high into the Pyrenees it had been a joy to walk through beautiful scenery and to pause among the spring flowers, filling my lungs with mountain air. But it had also been a gentle reminder that I too am a part of nature – a physical creature – breathing the same air and drinking the same water, even made of the same physical elements as all of God's creatures.

Lifestyles in the West, however, shelter us from the knowledge of our creatureliness. Our ability to import food supplies and to control indoor temperatures dulls our awareness of the seasons; abundance means that we are rarely hungry or thirsty or aware of our dependence upon the graciousness of the climate; sickness and tiredness are masked by drugs; and death is banished to institutions and to the edges of consciousness as medical advances prolong the life cycle. More often we see ourselves as the conquerors of nature. When we become aware of our dependence and our vulnerability, we interpret it as failure.

Although the Christian Scriptures define human beings as creatures first, much of Christian history has emphasized what differentiates human beings from other species, rather than what binds us to the rest of creation. Adam's naming of the animals in Genesis 2 has led to a hierarchical reading of the natural world, putting the land and other creatures at the disposal of human beings for their use. It is true that in recent times the language has changed from domination to stewardship, but even this masks the shared creatureliness of humans and other beings, allowing human beings still to feel in control.

Do you see yourself as a fellow creature with other animals?

Although parts of the Church, like the Franciscan tradition, have maintained a deep sense of the spirituality of creation and a sense of human kinship with the earth, it is rare for Christian churches to pay much attention to human creatureliness. Yet, for Christians, Adam is the figure

35

in whom humanity is summed up and his very name means earth creature. The name in which humanity is summed up indicates that human beings belong to the earth. We are made from the same carbons and hydrogens and oxygens and minerals that make up the rivers and the mountains. Even our brains are physical, made of the same elements as all organic matter; even these shall return to nourish the earth. In a world where human activity threatens the life of the planet, getting in touch with our creatureliness can help us to develop a proper sense of humility and proportion.

The Latin word for humility comes from the same root as 'humus', soil. Being grounded in our creatureliness, knowing that we are not self-made people, is the appropriate grammar of our conversation with God. It is knowing that we are creatures, interconnected with the whole of creation and dependent for life, not upon our own ingenuity, but upon God, which enables a discourse with God which is based in reality. This is part of the wisdom of the creation stories of the book of Genesis. Eve and Adam behave in the garden of Eden as if they are not creatures but gods in their own right, and eat the fruit of the tree which is forbidden to them. Immediately their relationship with God becomes awkward. They realize their nakedness and go into hiding. Part of our coming out of hiding is realizing that we are creatures, grounded, belonging to the earth, made of clay, breathed into life by the breath of the Spirit of God. This is humility – knowing the ground of our being is not ourselves, but God.

Being grounded in our creatureliness is the appropriate grammar of our conversation with God.

Such knowledge is not deducible from the world in itself and yet placing ourselves on the edge of civilization in a remote place can help us to be attentive to the God who made us. Allowing ourselves to drink water from the same source as wild mountain cattle can help us to absorb more deeply our humanity and live content in our creatureliness, without reaching out to try to grasp what does not belong to us, what we cannot change and what cannot make us happy. Coming to the end of our own physical resources is another, and rather less gentle, reminder of our creatureliness, and perhaps this is a more familiar motif of traditional literature about pilgrimage.

On the road, after the first few springing miles the backpack begins to bite; the blisters begin to form; the cold of the morning mist begins to eat into the bones. Then at the end of the day, the softness of a bed is so welcome; the sensation of rubbing ibuprofen gel into the shoulders is heavenly; the hands of a friend attending to blisters and massaging away the weariness of the feet brings the pilgrim near to tears. In this way the natural world in the form of the pilgrim's own body becomes a mode of disclosure whereby we can grow into a more mature understanding of our limits as human beings.

At times like these, in pain and in its relief, I was reminded of James Nelson's words, 'If we do not know the gospel in our bodies, we do not know the gospel. We either experience God's presence in our bodies or not at all.'[4] Christian faith may at times make the mistake of spiritualizing our material life as if it were something to be escaped, and yet Christians celebrate the mystery that God is to be known primarily through incarnation – in Augustine's words – as an 'intimacy in our flesh'. Incarnation is not just about a historical event – the life of one man – it is about the profound truth that we experience God most profoundly when we are most human. Each human body, to use Luther's term, becomes a 'mask of God'.

Perhaps this is something about which the medieval church knew more than contemporary western Christians generally do. For medieval pilgrims, physical hardship was an important part of the journey which would take them to the edge of themselves and open them to God's grace. The body was a gateway to God's grace. In the western world our relationships with our bodies waver between indulging them and then covering up what they really look like. We are either in love with our bodies and the pleasure they can afford us or punitive towards them, wishing they were more perfect than they are. So, in the Sunday papers today, 'pilgrimages without the pain' are openly advertised as a good thing. Pain is only acceptable in the service of making the body more perfect rather than in discovering its limits. What it is difficult for western Christians to do is to treat the body as if it were part of us; a mode of our identity which reveals both how vulnerable we are and how capable of receiving care and love.

The body is a gateway to God's grace.

Before I went on pilgrimage I assumed that the traditions of fasting and self-denial with which penance is associated in my mind were intended to focus the mind on higher things. Yet my experience of physical hardship was that I became more aware of my body rather than less, and more aware of it, not as something to escape, but as an occasion for grace.

As I went to bed, high in the Pyrenees, little did I know how soon I was to discover my own physical limits. Yet in the night the wind came up; shutters banged and the furniture on the terrace was thrown into the air. Although by the morning the weather had settled enough for our host to reassure us that it was safe to travel, we were only a couple of miles on our way before the wind became a real force to be reckoned with. Pilgrims began to be tossed about on the path like bits of debris. Following winds pushed us breathlessly uphill; swirling winds plucked hats and glasses and gloves from pockets and sent them plummeting down the mountain; crosswinds left us lying face down on the road, afraid to go forwards or to return.

I have never before experienced physical conditions that I simply could not overcome or escape. I could feel the wind catching my rucksack and whipping me from side to side on the road. I began to think that I might be one of those pilgrims whose crosses would be erected on these mountains. Between gusts, we crawled forwards; through wind tunnels, we held hands; feet and hands and faces went numb; legs started to ache and plead for rest; the snow got deeper and the mist denser and now we could not see where we had come from or where we were headed.

Now I felt like a pilgrim in a barren land. Now, I knew myself to be a creature – mortal and vulnerable – but now the knowledge was not a relief, but terrifying. As the wind stripped my pockets and whipped my face, I felt pruned of the illusions of control and self-reliance that I can get away with in much of my life. I began to realize that any conception of myself that does not take my physicality seriously is a fantasy.

Yet maintaining faith in God before this storm was not a simple matter. Did I believe that in this wind God was stripping me of illusions? Was I to see it as a slight, momentary affliction, trusting that the God who loves me does not punish me but prunes me for my own good? Was I to believe that God was in control of the wind and that if I prayed the wind would stop or, at least, God would save me?

My senses told me otherwise. Although the day before, nature had seemed benign and renewing, today it had become terrifying in its power, impersonal and merciless. There would be no special pleading before this wind. Now nature seemed not to be aligned with God but a chaotic force let loose and out of control.

Perhaps it is experiences like these, and those which happen to humanity on a grander scale, which make it difficult for us to speak about God as creator and ourselves as creatures. It is easy to become romantic and sentimental about the natural world, especially for those of us who live in towns and cities and who fantasize about a more earthed way of life. Yet anyone who works out in the weather or with animals knows that nature can not only be beautiful but random and capricious. Medieval pilgrims who waited, sometimes for weeks, for a companion with whom to cross the Pyrenees, were keenly aware that God and nature are not always aligned.

So a credible belief in God as creator must be able to hold together both the beauty and the capriciousness of nature. God cannot naively be identified with the beautiful sunset and then, artibrarily, be held to play no part in the destructive storm. To move beyond this impasse, we need to revisit our understanding of God's action in the natural world; to establish a more biblical understanding than those which have prevailed since Darwin published his *Origin of Species*. If we believe in Darwin's theory of natural selection, then we tend to read Genesis as a metaphorical account of the world which has more to do with its purpose than with its origins. For many people, if a notion of God is entertained at all, it is as a remote initiator of the evolutionary process. This God does not interfere with the laws of nature and therefore cannot be expected to relate to the world in a continuing way. Such a God only influences the world spiritually through the minds of human beings, or else only intervenes miraculously according to an arbitrary scheme of his own or when prayer has been fervent enough.

Yet, the biblical witness suggests that the act of creation was not merely a one-time initiative nor a detached experiment, but a labour of love by which the universe is sustained in being every minute; an understanding which is not only metaphorical but actual. In creating, God does not retain control over creation, any more than over human creatures. Each created thing has its integrity and freedom which opens the natural world to potential tragedy. Yet, in creating, God does not withdraw from the natural world, nor lose the initiative. In movements of grace, the three persons of the Trinity – source, spirit and word – are continually at work, influencing the creation for good and drawing all things together with those that love God (Romans 8.28). In the same chapter of Romans Paul makes clear that the redemption God offers is for the whole created order. God is intimately present, not only to human beings, but to all reality, all of the time.

This view is distinct from a pantheist belief that God is indistinguishable from material things – God was not the storm that nearly blew me off the mountain. But neither does this view associate the activity of God only with the beautiful. From this perspective, although God was not the storm and although God's character cannot be deduced from the storm, yet God's grace can be communicated through the storm. God and I can meet if I am open to the encounter.

Open to encounter

What I experienced on the mountain was profoundly frightening, and yet it opened the cells of my being to encounter truths about myself, about others and about God.

The relief of reaching the Collado Lepoeder at 1600m was enormous – from there we could see the monastery of Roncesvalles nestling in the valley below. But as I trekked down the mountainside, delighted again by the narcissus emerging from the rocky soil, what I brought down with me was a sense of an unlimitable God who communicates with his people through all manner of means and whose presence hovers beneath the surface of things, ready to break out into our experience. That evening, as I attended Mass in the monastery, I thought about the bread and the wine and how God communicates with us through these physical things. Here, too, there seemed a sense that God is ready to disclose himself through material things if we are open to his presence.

The bread and wine of Communion suggest a God who discloses himself through material things if we are open to his presence.

The biblical narrative is full of examples of God bursting into encounter through material things: a burning bush, the sound of silence, mud and spittle, or simply the touch of a cloak. These stories disclose a God who reveals himself through material and physical means – whose presence is tangible to those with faith to reach out and touch him.

In the days that followed the ordeal on the mountain, the scenery was much more gentle than that of the Pyrenees, although the weather closed in again. As we walked down through the foothills of Navarre into Pamplona and on towards Logroño, repeatedly I was struck with a profound sense of God's presence and self-communication through the material world. It happened, again, much later, as I approached the penultimate stage of the Camino. I had spent the morning climbing towards the Cruz de Hierro at the highest point of the route and I was looking for a place to have lunch and a siesta. Something beckoned me off the path and led me to a waterfall, not visible from the Camino. It was a hot day and immediately I took off my boots and socks, ready to immerse them in the cold running water. Yet as I did it, it seemed that this was no simple meeting of physical need, but an occasion for grace – almost a foot-washing by Christ himself – and I bent and kissed the water in gratitude.

Have you ever been put in touch with God through a physical sensation?

I am certain that the Camino lends itself to such experiences because it is a storied place. Those who walk here are alert to the presence of God because others have met him here before. When I set off I imagined it would be churches and shrines and public places associated with the religious experience of the past that would provide occasion for spiritual experience. As I walked and talked with others along the way, I became more confident that any bush or tree or waterfall may become an occasion for encounter with God if we trust that God remains intimately connected with the natural world.

If we are confident that God remains intimately connected with the natural world, any bush, tree or waterfall may become an occasion for encounter.

Through a sometimes barren and often beautiful land, the Camino offers time and space in which to become attentive to the physical and natural world. Its challenge is that we learn the truth of our own creatureliness and come to experience the ordinary things of the material world as arenas for encounter with the God who sustains it in being. However, slowing down, paying attention to physical sensations, delighting in the world and expecting God to communicate through it, are disciplines which belong in the daily practice of the Christian life. As we organize our diaries, we might take time to walk from place to place, taking in the details of the world around us. As we read Scripture we might pay more attention to the physical elements of the stories by which we live – letting rocks and stones and trees and flowers come alive with God's presence. In worship we might broaden our use of symbols and meditate on their physical characteristics: handling salt and oil and clay and ashes might put us more in touch with our creatureliness and with our creator. Finally a closer attention to the material things we use – in worship, industry and in our daily lives – might help us, not only to join in God's delight in the world, but to grieve where it is damaged or under threat and to align ourselves in practical ways with the movements of grace and love through which God is redeeming the entire earth.

Day 1
And it was very good

God saw everything that he had made, and indeed, it was very good. And there was evening and there was morning, the sixth day. Thus the heavens and the earth were finished, and all their multitude.

Genesis 1.31-2.1

Living life at walking pace in the open air opens the pilgrim's eyes to the sights and sounds of the natural world. The changing weather, birds in flight, farm animals grazing, even frogs basking in the sunshine can be a source of delight.

According to Genesis, when God made the world he expressed delight in everything he had made. In the busyness of contemporary life perhaps it is only children who, unselfconsciously, have the time and emotional space to be surprised and delighted by the natural world. Yet to delight in God's creatures is to be drawn into God's delight in all that is made. To experience delight is to become more like God.

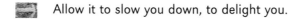 Spend some time being present to the detail of a creature or plant.

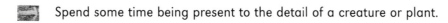 Allow it to slow you down, to delight you.

Human beings are used to reading Genesis as if the rest of the natural world were for our use, and yet each species has its own integrity and beauty and relatedness to the creator. What is needed is a recovered sense that we, like other earth creatures, belong to the land and are interdependent with our fellow creatures. Only then shall we be able to listen to other members of the earth community and learn from their wisdom.

One of the things that other creatures can teach us is the delight that comes from being fully ourselves. There is much pleasure in watching a dog run at top speed for the sheer joy of it, or seeing a flower open to the sun because that is what it is made to do. To be fully ourselves is perhaps the most fundamental way of worshipping God – glorifying God by being the creatures we were created to be.

 When are you most completely alive?

 Might this be the worship God most desires from you?

All things praise thee, Lord most high;
Heaven and earth and sea and sky,
All were for thy glory made,
That thy greatness thus displayed
Should all worship bring to thee;
All things praise thee, Lord, may we[5].

Day 2

Don't you sense me?

Does not wisdom call,
and does not understanding raise her voice?
When there were no depths I was brought forth,
when there were no springs abounding with water.
When he established the heavens I was there,
when he drew a circle on the face of the deep,
then I was beside him, like a master worker;
and I was daily his delight.
And now, my children, listen to me:
happy are those who keep my ways.

Proverbs 8.1, 24, 27, 30, 32

The Wisdom tradition within Scripture suggests that the world was made by wisdom; that wisdom is at the heart of the universe and is almost tangible if we will recognize ourselves as part of creation and listen to the wisdom that made it. Such a vision of God suggests that the world is almost God's body: that by touching any part of the physical world, we might encounter God's very self.

Throughout the Bible God remains intimately connected with created, material things. There is a persistent sense in the biblical narrative that any tree or bush or stream may become an occasion for God's self-disclosure.

 Go into the garden and bury your hands in the soil or take off your shoes and walk on some grass or by the sea; look at the sky and breathe deeply.

 Allow God to speak to you through your senses.

In the life of the Church, a sense that God communicates with us in physical ways is maintained through the sacraments of Holy Communion and baptism, where ordinary physical things – water, wine and bread – become the occasion for meeting with God. In these sacraments we express the faith that God lives just beneath the surface of all physical things ready to break into our experience. To live sacramentally is to live in the world as those who believe that at any moment we might find ourselves on holy ground. It is to be alert to the presence of God through our senses.

Embodied God,
in touch with the whole creation,
speaking in rushing wind and tongues of flame,
speak to us through our senses
that we may live and breathe and grow
into the creatures you made us at our making.
Amen.

Day 3
The force of the storm

God is our refuge and strength,
a very present help in trouble.
Therefore we will not fear, though the earth should change,
though the mountains shake in the heart of the sea;
though its waters roar and foam,
though the mountains tremble with its tumult.

Psalm 46.1-3

A pilgrimage on foot across rugged terrain will at some point remind the pilgrim of their smallness and physical vulnerability. It can literally bring the pilgrim to their knees. If we believe, deep down, that the world is capricious and may trample us underfoot, then small and modest on the ground is not a place we can bear to be. If we believe, deep down, that what God wants is to cut us down to size and punish us for our presumption we would be right to resist. Only if we believe that the power in the universe is good and on our side can we afford to take the risk of being present to our vulnerability as human beings, trusting that this will be an occasion for grace.

When the psalmists are overwhelmed by trouble, they begin by articulating their feelings of smallness and abandonment to God. Often these feelings are expressed in the language of storms. They speak of high winds, or of drowning at sea, or of earthquakes shaking the foundations of the earth. Although these are powerful metaphors for the storms of life, they also reflect terror at the merciless power of nature.

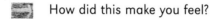 Think of a time when the power of nature has overwhelmed you.

 How did this make you feel?

The psalmists often begin with feelings of abandonment in the face of a storm, and yet as they persist in prayer their confidence that they are held and heard, despite the tumult around them, grows.

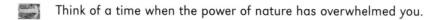 How do you feel about bringing your own feelings of smallness and abandonment to God?

Lord our God,
when our confidence in our own strength is shaken,
strengthen our faith in you.
When our faith in your goodness is tested,
be good for us,
as your grace ripens within us.
Amen.

Day 4
Body matters

I am poured out like water,
and all my bones are
    out of joint;
my heart is like wax;
it is melted within my breast;
my mouth is dried up
    like a potsherd,
and my tongue sticks
    to my jaws;
you lay me in the dust
    of death.

Psalm 22.14–15

A pilgrimage cannot happen if you do not take care of your physical needs. Even so, the repetitive action of walking on stony roads for weeks makes huge demands on even the most hardened of feet. The pain of blisters brings the pilgrim in touch with their limits. There are times when the body cannot go any further, and the insistent mind must listen to the body's needs, and allow them to be met.

The needs of the body can be treated as an inconvenience, or angrily rejected as evidence of weakness, but they also can be seen as a way of receiving the truth that we are not invulnerable. The purpose of our physical vulnerability is not that we learn the pain of humiliation, but that we open ourselves to receive the knowledge that we are beloved.

The words of this psalmist arise from physical exhaustion and dehydration. They speak of a body in distress; a body which is even close to death. It is often in times of physical illness that we become aware of our bodies, not as machines which house our essential selves, but as fundamental aspects of what it is to be human. It is through our bodies that we know both pain and care. The importance of the physical body is expressed in the Christian belief in the resurrection of the body. Just as Christ's resurrection body bears the scars of the crucifixion, so we shall carry our embodied knowledge of pain and grace beyond the grave into a transfigured life.

- Think about a time when your body has needed care.

- How able were you to receive that care as knowledge that you are beloved?

In many Christian churches bodily gestures are part of the way in which grace is appropriated and experienced.

- Try kneeling to pray or holding out your hands to receive that for which you ask.

- Try making the sign of the cross on your forehead with water to remember your baptism or anointing your hands with oil.

- Pay attention to the physical sensations you experience and allow them to become channels of grace.

You anoint my head with oil; my cup overflows.
Surely goodness and mercy shall follow me all the days of my life.
Psalm 23.5,6.

Day 5

In returning and rest you shall be saved

And on the seventh day God finished the work that he had done, and he rested on the seventh day from all the work he had done. So God blessed the seventh day and hallowed it, because on it God rested from all the work that he had done in creation.

Genesis 2.2–3

Pilgrimage offers a rhythm of work and rest. Some of the work is the physical business of walking: the calves pulling as the body climbs uphill; the strain in the knees of walking downhill with a heavy pack. Some of the work is emotional as the pilgrim learns to bear the company of others they are finding difficult, or to bear their own company. In the evening the pilgrim rests from all this work in order to renew body, mind, soul and strength for the journey ahead.

The rhythm of work and rest is a wisdom of which the Bible speaks in the language of Sabbath. For the Jewish people this was not a freedom restricted, but sabbatical time in which to be present to the God who gives life, and time to remember that the world is not held in being by our activity but by the loving embrace of God. A 24/7 society offers the freedom to work or engage in leisure activities at all times of the day and night, yet our pursuit of pleasure can be as exhausting as our work. Without the imposed discipline of Sunday rest, how can we give one another permission to stop and simply be?

 What does the notion of Sabbath or sabbatical suggest to you?

 Are there ways in which you might need to alter the rhythm of your life to receive God's gift of rest?

Try relaxing your body as you pray:

> lie on the floor or sit in a comfortable chair;
> become aware of your body;
> tense each part in turn and then relax it;
> with each breath, breathe in the goodness of God;
> with each breath, breathe out all tension and anxiety.

'Be still and know that I am God.'

Thou bringest all again; with thee
  Is light, is space, is breadth and room
For each thing, fair, beloved and free
  To have its hour of life and bloom.[6]

Day 6

The whole creation

The Camino passes through parts of rural Spain where subsistence farmers still own a few cows and sheep. In this picture an elderly woman and her dog takes her animals to find pasture.

Remember the Sabbath day, and keep it holy. For six days you shall labour and do all your work. But the seventh day is a Sabbath to the LORD your God; you shall not do any work – you, your son or your daughter, your male or female slave, your livestock, or the alien resident in your towns. For in six days the LORD made heaven and earth, the sea and all that is in them, but rested the seventh day; therefore the LORD blessed the Sabbath day and consecrated it.

Exodus 20.8–11

In Scripture the Sabbath is not just for the people of Israel, but for the whole creation. Employees and slaves and animals and even the land itself is entitled to rest. If pilgrimage provides a retreat from the 24/7 society it also provides a critique of it. Not only pilgrims, but the whole creation would benefit from a more natural rhythm of work and rest.

In a complex global economy it is no simple matter to live out sabbatical principles which deliver justice for the land, for livestock and for the poor of the earth. Yet the Old and New Testaments agree that salvation is not simply for the faithful few, but for the whole creation. Those who are in tune with the God who created the world and holds it in being, will groan with the whole creation, lamenting any damage done to it, and seeking to live justly within it.

 Think about the impact upon the earth of the way you live. Make a change in the amount of waste you produce. What can be recycled? What can be composted?

 Think about the cost of the products you buy to those whose labour has produced them. Ask your supermarket to stock more Fairtrade food, drinks and clothing.

With the whole creation
We cry to the Lord: Lord, have mercy.
With waters that glisten with oil and dead fish
We cry to the Lord: Lord, have mercy.
With ice that has melted and coastlines flooded
We cry to the Lord: Lord, have mercy.
With forests felled and soils now denuded
We cry to the Lord: Lord, have mercy.
With creatures extinct and peoples displaced
We cry to the Lord: Lord, have mercy.
With the whole creation
We yearn for redemption: Lord, grant us peace.

53

3: Christ the Pilgrim
– from Logroño to Burgos

This sculpture of a naked pilgrim wearing only the scallop shell of St James sits in the cathedral square in Burgos.

From Logroño to Burgos

I walked the road from Logroño to Burgos in the company of two friends who flew out from Cambridge to join me. Having told them that the weather by now could be quite hot, they had come with high hopes of a suntan, but what they came to was rain, and more rain, and mud. The region through which we were walking was La Rioja, and the mud of La Rioja is red. The soil is fertile and supports the vines which produce the famous wines of the region, but it clumps onto the pilgrim's boots, making progress along the path slow and heavy. At times it was so much like wading through treacle that we resorted to following the main road, braving the fumes and the splashback of passing lorries in preference to disappearing into the clay without trace.

I had hoped for a brighter start for my companions whose first experience of the Camino this was. Yet by the time we were approaching Nájera where we hoped to find a bed for the night, they had already been through enough to be able to resonate with these words of graffiti splashed on a factory wall by a passing pilgrim:

> *Dust, mud, sun and rain*
> *Form the way to Santiago.*
> *Thousands of pilgrims*
> *And more than a thousand years.*
>
> *Pilgrim, who calls you?*
> *What hidden force draws you?*
> *Not the field of stars*
> *Nor the grand cathedrals;*
> *Not majestic Navarre*
> *Nor the wines of La Rioja;*
> *Not the seafood of Galicia*
> *Nor the plains of Castille ...*
>
> *All these I see as I pass by*
> *And they are a joy to see,*
> *But the voice which calls to me*
> *I sense more deeply.*
> *The force that pulls me,*
> *The force that draws me*
> *I cannot explain.*
> *Only the one, above, can know.*[7]

My companions had seen enough mud in one day to identify with the first line of the poem, but already they also both had a sense that although the sights and sounds along the way might offer great richness, it is not the journey outwards alone which makes the Camino, but the journey inwards, the journey into God.

It is not the journey outwards alone which makes a pilgrimage but the journey inwards, the journey into God.

For the graffiti artist this God is unnamed – simply the 'One Above'. For the Christian, the One Above is the God we see in Jesus Christ – the God who not only draws us onwards towards the heavenly city – but who comes out to meet us and travels with us along our way. The Christian belief that God walks alongside us on the journey of our life is illustrated in the story of Jesus walking with the two disciples along the Emmaus road (Luke 24.13–35).

The two disciples are walking away from Jerusalem after the crucifixion. They are despondent and cannot believe that the stranger they encounter does not know what has taken place in the last few days. They explain their misery and their dashed hopes as the stranger gently prompts them to speak about the heaviness of their hearts. It is only when Jesus has walked with them and listened to them and allowed them to tell their story that he begins to speak himself, explaining the necessity for the Son of Man to suffer before he could enter into his glory. Yet still he does not reveal himself to them. Not until they have invited him into their home does his identity become clear as he completes the familiar action of breaking the bread.

The story demonstrates Jesus' willingness to journey with us, to travel the route we are taking, to listen to our concerns, to help us gently to name the depth of our need. Only when we are confident we are being listened to and taken seriously does Jesus begin to speak. When he does, our perspective begins to change. In fact, in this story, the disciples' perspective changes so much that they change direction completely and head back towards Jerusalem, not dragging their feet as they were before, but running with light hearts and bursting with good news.

Walking the Camino does not involve such U-turns. The direction is always towards the holy city. Yet sometimes the way feels heavy and lonely and the heart is full of all that weighs it down. The pilgrim is ready to sigh, with the disciples on the Emmaus road, 'we had hoped', and perhaps is ready to give up. In the week that the three of us walked from Logroño to Burgos, there were certainly times when each of us felt weary and despairing, yet there were also moments of enlightenment when it seemed that we did not walk alone but were accompanied, not just by each other, but by the presence of Christ.

The Emmaus story demonstrates God's willingness to travel with us.

On our fourth day together, as we came over the Oca Mountains from Villafranca de Montes de Oca towards the monastery of San Juan de Ortega, one of my companions lagged behind. Afterwards she wrote:

> *Wrapped in a cloud of despondency I plod on,*
> *Pouring out the feelings of failure and abandonment*
> *To the pilgrim, present,*

And yet veiled from view,
Who walks beside me patiently,
Mile after mile.
Only later do I stop to wonder, to marvel
At the presence that would not desert me,
And how, obsessed with fears,
I nearly missed his words of love.[8]

As in the Emmaus story our ability to recognize the veiled companion who walks with us even when everyone else has deserted us is often delayed. We realize as we look back and sometimes the realization comes as a flash of recognition. As I walked across those mountains and I encountered the barren landscapes of my own fears and obsessions within, it was not until I reached the cathedral city of Burgos that I recognized the Christ who had been walking with me.

Looking back can you identify times when silently Christ has been walking with you?

The naked pilgrim

In Burgos the yellow arrows take the pilgrim right into the cathedral square. Its white stone towers pierce the sky; storks balance precariously on the pinnacles and vie with the stone angels for attention. I sat upon a bench to rest my legs and enjoy the scene. Seated next to me was a naked pilgrim. A statue in bronze, he has nothing to identify him but the pilgrim's shell and staff and water gourd. Apart from that he is completely naked. His feet are horribly blistered and scarred and his spine is exposed to the gaze of everyone as it protrudes through his emaciated skin.

Whether this statue was intended by its sculptor to represent a particular pilgrim, racked with the leprosy that was not uncommon among those who undertook this pilgrimage in medieval times; or every pilgrim, stripped bare by the discipline of the road, is open to interpretation. I saw myself – his feet, painful and glad to be unencumbered by boots, were my feet; his bones, exposed to the world reflected how raw and near the surface I felt my deepest self to be. Yet, he was not just me – in his body I saw pilgrims throughout the ages, travelling along these roads, experiencing these states of body and mind. Thousands before have worked out their salvation under these skies, among these stones. In his body they were all summed up, and I felt one with them. But beyond that, in his body, I saw the whole of humanity – particularly those who suffer – but all of us in our vulnerability and mortality, however well we hide it. The whole of humanity seemed gathered up in those exposed bones.

My ability to recognize myself in this pilgrim statue was focused around the scallop shell which both he and I were wearing, for the scallop shell is the symbol of the pilgrimage to Santiago. Traditionally pilgrims are thought to have picked up these shells on the beach at Finisterre a few days' walk beyond the holy city. Having reached Santiago, they would go on to the 'end of the earth', burning their clothes and collecting shells as souvenirs. Alternatively the story goes that when the body of St James was transported from Palestine to Santiago, it came by sea. Falling into the water one day, his body was rescued by angels, and when it was dragged back into the boat it was covered in scallops. Whatever the origin of the association, these days, the shells are sold at the side of the road with strings attached ready to wear. Mine, I had picked up from the beach in my home town of Dover and had carried with me all the way to Spain. On the journey, with its worn edges, barnacles and scratches, it had come to represent my life: my origins, my growing up, my achievements and disappointments; and all I had been through on this pilgrimage: all I had witnessed, all those I had met, all I had confronted in myself, all I had yet to learn.

The shell had come to represent my deepest self, opened by the rigours of the road. As I encountered myself, I identified with all who had ever worn this shell: both my contemporaries and those who in previous generations had worked out their salvation under these skies, among these stones. Seeing this naked pilgrim wearing nothing but the shell broadened the association further – here was all humanity in our vulnerability.

As I sat on the bench I looked down at my boots, still caked in mud, and I remembered the redness of the soil that weighed down our feet as we walked out of Logroño towards Najera. In the book of Genesis, when God creates humanity, he does so out of the clay – Adam means 'earth person' but the Hebrew word, *adamah*, also means red. In the story of creation, although Adam is the first person, his role is to represent all people – the terracotta people – made from the red dust of the earth.

Sitting beside this naked pilgrim in the square at Burgos – a figure made first of terracotta and then cast in bronze – I saw Adam, dressed in the universal clay of humanity, yet my overwhelming sense was of Christ, becoming clay for us: a God who is literally wearing my clothes and is actually human. I felt the exposed bone of his back – it felt not just like meeting myself or any another vulnerable human being, but touching the Word made flesh, touching God's very self. The first letter of John puts it like this:

> *We declare to you what was from the beginning, what we have heard, what we have*
> *seen with our eyes, what we have looked at and touched with*
> *our hands, concerning the word of life. (1 John 1.1)*

The extraordinary claim at the heart of the gospel is that God has chosen to be identified with us in flesh and blood.

What became clear to me in the square in Burgos was that whenever we are in touch with the vulnerability of another person, or our own, simultaneously, we are connected with God in Christ, whether we know it or not.

Central to Christian doctrine is the statement from the Nicene Creed that Christ was both fully human and fully God. Resting my head on this pilgrim statue, I could see what the Word made flesh had got to do with me. It was not simply that here I was sitting on a bench with a fellow pilgrim. It was not even that here I recognized the God who walks alongside us, patiently waiting for us to recognize him. The power of the image was in the realization that in Christ, God himself has become like me, taking on all the implications of human vulnerability in order that I might come to know that my home, like his, is in the company of God. Because I was already identified with the image of the pilgrim and with pilgrims throughout the ages, this image of the naked pilgrim gave me access to the extraordinary claim at the heart of the Christian gospel that the God who is the ground of our being has chosen to be identified with us in flesh and blood:

> *God, the blest, the great I AM,*
> *Sojourns in this vale of tears,*
> *And Jesus is his name.*

Charles Wesley's Christmas hymn uses the rather old-fashioned word, 'sojourns'. It is an important concept in the Hebrew scriptures which suggests, not a brief visit to a foreign country, but the patient, long-term commitment to live with another people and to make them your own as, for example, Ruth did with Naomi's people. In the context of the Christian gospel, the image emphasizes the importance of Christ's humanity. This is not God on holiday, seeming to be human. In Christ, God stands solidly in the shoes of the human race, that we might recognize ourselves in him.

How difficult do you find it to see what Jesus has to do with you?

One of the things which some contemporary people find very difficult to understand about Christianity is how one life or death can affect the whole human race. As one fellow pilgrim put it to me, 'I can see that if God made everything, God made me, but what has the life of a centuries-old rabbi to do with me?' In western culture we are so convinced of our individuality that we are more aware of ourselves as separate from the rest of the human race than identified with it. Christian faith suggests that by committing ourselves to enter deeply into our own particular experience of being human, we discover our profound connection with the whole human race which, in Christ, is at one with God.

Pilgrimage, as we saw in the last chapter, opens human beings up to the embodiment and mortality which we all share. In doing so it makes an opportunity for contemporary people to identify, not just with other pilgrims, but with the whole human race. Whether Christ seems to us to have anything to do with any of this will partly depend on how able we are to allow our pictures of Jesus to be fully human.

Pilgrimage makes an opportunity for contemporary people to identify with all of humanity and so with Christ.

Often, the gospels are preached as if Jesus had a divine programme in his head – as if he did not have real choices to make; as if he did not struggle with the call of God; as if he never smiled or laughed or wept; as if his betrayal, torture and death were not fully experienced; as if he did not suffer appalling pain, dereliction and abandonment; as if he was not fully human. The Early Church

Fathers, however, were acutely aware of the importance of Christ's humanity: if Jesus only seemed to be human and was not really one of us, subject to the same trials, joys and temptations, then there are dimensions of human experience which still remain outside the scope of God – there are aspects of our experience which can separate us from God. By contrast, Christ's full humanity proclaims that there is nothing in all creation which can separate us from the love of God (Romans 8.35–39).

For human beings to recognize themselves in Christ, they must engage with his humanity. Our embarrassment about aspects of our own human vulnerability, however, pushes us towards covering up his. A good example is our embodiment. To see a completely naked human statue in any city square is for many in bad taste, even if it is a perfect specimen. To see the image of an 'imperfect' human being evokes enormous ambivalence. To name this image, Christ, is to make him more human than most of us are conventionally comfortable with.

Yet, if we are to appreciate the depth of God's identification with us in Jesus, we need images that help us to appropriate our own humanity and recognize it as so profoundly lovable and loved that God would become enfleshed, taking the risk of incarnation, even of torture and death. The challenge for the Church in every generation and culture is to find ways of presenting this central mystery of the Christian faith that will enable people to find kinship with God in Christ and understand that they are one with him.

The challenge for the Church in every generation is to enable people to find kinship with God in Christ.

Christ the Pilgrim

Given the popularity of pilgrim imagery in the way that people today are describing the journey of life, and the resurgence of interest in actual pilgrimages, it may be that the image of Christ the Pilgrim has something to offer the churches as they seek to communicate God's longing for humanity's wholeness.

Although Jesus was never a pilgrim to Santiago, he was a pilgrim to Jerusalem on more than one occasion. He knew what it was to be part of a long journey and a company of pilgrims travelling together focused on a holy city. We know this from the story of his being left behind at the age of 12, and by his presence in Jerusalem at the time of various festivals. In some ways his final journey to Jerusalem for the Passover was a pilgrimage, all the way from the Mount of Transfiguration. It was a physical journey, but also an inward journey, into the heart of what he believed his Father was calling him to do.

These concrete instances give us some sense of Jesus the Pilgrim, but the point of presenting Jesus in this way is to suggest that his whole life was a pilgrimage – a journey of self-emptying, becoming human, journeying through death that humanity might follow with him into life. The journey is spelt out by Paul in Philippians 2.5–7:

The whole of Jesus' life was a pilgrimage – a journey of self-emptying – that humanity might follow him through death into life.

Let the same mind be in you that was in Christ Jesus,
who, though he was in the form of God,
did not regard equality with God
as something to be exploited,
but emptied himself,
taking the form of a slave,
being born in human likeness.
And being found in human form,
he humbled himself
and became obedient to the point of death –
even death on a cross.
Therefore God also highly exalted him
and gave him the name
that is above every name.

Using pilgrimage to describe the journey of the Word into human flesh is not as recent an idea as the contemporary sculpture of the naked pilgrim would suggest. In the monastery of Santo Domingo at Silos, just south of Burgos, there is a series of eleventh-century friezes. The whole sequence depicts Christ's sojourn on the earth, but in the portrayal of Christ on the road to Emmaus, the nature of this journey as a pilgrimage is made explicit.

Christ the Pilgrim not only accompanies us on our journey but seeks to draw us onto the life-giving road he has forged.

Here, Christ is dressed in medieval pilgrim costume, and as the guidebook says, 'con extraordinaria libertad', he wears the scallop shell that identifies any pilgrim on their way to the shrine of St James.

I made the detour off the Camino from Burgos in order to stand in front of this image. Dressed, myself, in the scallop shell of the pilgrim to Santiago, it was like looking into a mirror. In some ways the image is anachronistic. It is a projection of the medieval pilgrim identity onto Christ, but as a means of helping me to recognize myself in Christ it was invaluable. Here was Christ, wearing the shell that had come to mean so much to me. Here was one who in life had engaged literally in pilgrimages to Jerusalem, and metaphorically in a journey of faith through the wilderness to the cross and who now, risen, wearing the scallop shell badge of one who has completed the pilgrimage, was coming to meet me on the way, inviting me into the life of God, offering me all the fullness of God.

I had gone to Silos to see this one image. But, there, in the cloisters, I found myself surrounded by eleventh-century sculptures of Christ, demonstrating his humanity through the intimate details of his body: his ribcage, his braided hair, his eyes boring into mine. As I gazed back I knew that I wanted my humanity to be transformed by his. I realized that the identification goes two ways. God, in Christ identifies with us, so that we may identify with him and so be transformed (2 Thessalonians 5.9–10; 2 Corinthians 3.18). Now, it was not just that I wanted Christ to walk alongside me, accompanying me and listening to me and comforting me on whatever road I have taken. Now I wanted to be drawn into the life-giving way that is the way of Christ.

Pilgrimage into Christ

Shocked by the immediacy of these thousand-year-old figures, I stepped back from my intense examination of each scene, and realized that the scenes from Jesus' life were in sequence: his birth, his death and resurrection; his appearance on the road to Emmaus; the encounter with doubting Thomas; the ascension; Pentecost. The figures are simple, square and crude yet they portray a profound intimacy between Christ and his followers that draw the onlooker into the story and invite the believer to make a pilgrimage into his life.

The ability of these scenes to draw those who look into the way of Christ is not an accident. Spaced around the cloister they function as a series of prayer stations, not unlike the stations of the cross that became popular later in the Middle Ages and which can be seen in most Roman Catholic and Anglican churches today. The cloister at Silos operated as a mini pilgrimage route – not unlike a contemporary labyrinth – inviting the monks and their guests to identify with the life of Christ in the same way that pilgrims on the road to Santiago, a few miles away, were doing on a rather more extended scale.

A consistent theme running through the literature about Christian pilgrimage through the ages has been its purpose in helping the pilgrim to become more and more identified with Christ. Perhaps this is most easily seen in the case of pilgrimage to Jerusalem where those who retrace the steps of Jesus towards Golgotha are literally taking up their cross and following after him as they seek to discover the meaning of discipleship in their own lives.

But, whether it is following the Via Dolorosa in Jerusalem or the road to a lesser shrine like Santiago, the rigours of the journey which open up the pilgrim and the intensification of symbols towards the end of the road encourage the believer to immerse themselves more and more in the identity of Christ such that, by the end of the journey, the pilgrim is ready to say, with St Paul, '[I] have died, [and my] life is hidden with Christ in God' (Colossians 3.3).

Radical identification with Christ is also a consistent theme in the letters of Paul. He speaks not just about receiving Christ into our lives so that God can work through us, but uses the language of being 'in Christ'. For Paul, this is the implication of our baptism: 'Do you not know that all of us who were baptized into Christ Jesus have been baptized into his death? Therefore we have been buried with him by baptism into death, so that, just as Christ was raised from the dead by the glory of the Father, so we too might walk in newness of life' (Romans 6.3–4). It is not that personal identity is obliterated by being baptized into Christ, but an almost organic union is implied: we who are following through death into new life become members of his body. We are being filled with all the fullness of God (Ephesians 3.19).

What images, stories or activities have helped you to identify with Christ?

For St Paul, what mattered was that the Christian's identity was located in Christ. Once people had made the decision to be baptized into Christ, he urged them to trust in their new identity more and more, leaving behind the sin that belonged to their old lives and letting the Spirit of Christ transform their attitudes and behaviours. In Galatians Paul describes this as seeking the Jerusalem which is above (Galatians 4.26). Paul was not concerned with arguments about physical pilgrimage to Jerusalem or anywhere else, but he was concerned with finding means by which Christians might reinforce their identity in Christ.

Physical pilgrimage, because it allows the individual to experience the fact of their common humanity, opens up the possibility of understanding that Christ who has joined himself to the human race in general has something to do with me, in particular. This is the first step in Christian faith – realizing that God is for us, enough to become human and share our life and our death – to make this pilgrimage of life with us. But the second step matters too. Christ's becoming human is no mere endorsement of whatever direction we happen to be taking. Christ joins himself with humanity in order to lead us in the direction of abundant life.

From death to life

At times, as I walked along, although my feet were still heading in the direction of Santiago, my thoughts were dominated by fears and obsessions and grief. Sometimes the journey into myself was not one of increasing self-understanding but one of self-pity in which I did not want to choose life, but was happy with techniques for existence that were tried and tested. Sometimes I resorted to counting the miles. Sometimes, like the lame man at the pool of Bethesda, I was not really sure that I wanted to be made well.

On those days, or in those periods of our lives when we are not ready to face the fact that we are choosing paths that are less than life-giving or are simply wandering around in ever-decreasing circles, it is tempting to want companions who will go with us wherever we are going. It is easy to choose friends who will collude with us in diverting attention from the deep issues of our lives. Although the Emmaus story reveals to us the God who will journey with us, and listen to us even when we are in despair, Christ is never content merely to accompany us on the path to our own destruction.

In the story from Luke, Christ walks with us and listens to us and genuinely wants to know how we are seeing things, but his companionship is in order to lead us to new life. The stone frieze at Silos depicts this by presenting Christ as the one in the lead. From the other side of the grave of despair and hopelessness, the resurrected Christ offers the way to life. He wants, not just to accompany these disciples, but to transform their lives.

Only a conviction that God loves us for ourselves ought to allow God the kind of transformative power in our lives which Paul articulates as dying with Christ.

As human beings we are rightly cautious about the extent to which we allow others influence over our lives. Letting others in is a necessary but risky business in which boundaries are important.

63

Yet Christ is not another person who might harm us, not even a saintly one. In Christ we meet God's very self. Only a conviction that God loves us for ourselves and has identified with us because he loves us ought to allow God the kind of transformative power in our lives which Paul articulates as dying with Christ.

Christians believe that the root of our health as human beings is to be identified with the ground of our being who is pure love. Because it is God's very self who becomes human in Christ, to identify with Christ is not to risk being overwhelmed by another person, even one with our best interests at heart. To identify with Christ is to find ourselves loved beyond measure for the people we are. To identify with Christ is to know ourselves loved and safe in eternity.

If our image of God is of a remote and perfect being who requires us to journey towards him, identification is difficult. Yet in Christ, what we see is a God who has made the difficult and precarious journey towards us in order that we might go with him. For this reason it is helpful in Christian mission to begin with thinking about our own experiences in which we recognized God's coming to meet us and then find ways of opening these experiences up to others, rather than beginning with theoretical doctrines that emphasize God's remoteness and human sinfulness and run the risk of enslaving people to fear or alienating them from God by presenting him as a tyrannical judge or manipulative parent.

God's identification with us in Christ is already made. When God, in Christ, became human, he identified with the whole of humanity. All flesh is affected by the incarnation, not just Christians. What distinguishes Christians from others are those who have recognized in the story of Christ's sojourn among us that God and humanity belong together, and so have opened themselves up to the Spirit of Jesus, wanting to be identified with him.

Many attempts at mission begin with the sinfulness of humanity and seek to convince people of that. They are followed by a presentation of Jesus as the solution, through a technical process of atonement. If in Christ God has truly become part of humanity, however, perhaps what is needed is not a theoretical, but an experiential, approach. It was my experience on the road to Santiago that a deeper engagement with my own humanity in all its joy and pain became disclosive of God's very self in my flesh. It was a journey of recognition into the truth that baptism represents – that my own body is part of the body of Christ – Christ's body is my home. The realization was helped by the artistic presentations of Christ that I encountered along the way, as well as the opportunities for worship with others on a similar journey. The journey was not so much into cognitive assent to the doctrines of the Church, but into the depths of my own humanity where the connection between myself and Christ the Pilgrim seemed obvious. My own experience and my conversations with David, whom we met in the first chapter, and with other pilgrims along the way have convinced me that the gospel is not so much a set of propositions of which to be convinced but 'an invitation to join a pilgrimage of "unknowing" into the living heart of God'.[9]

64

What human beings need to learn to do is to trust God's choosing of us in our humanity and allow our home realities to be transformed by this love at the heart of the universe. Our home realities are our habitual ways of seeing the world, many of which were formed in us as small children. In childhood, the world and its meanings are mediated to us by those who parent us; we absorb their way of looking at the world and ourselves implicitly because we are scarcely separate from them. This is a bond which is highly emotionally charged because it is essential to our survival as infants. Our earliest and most fundamental layers of identity are established by seeing ourselves through the eyes of those who parent us. For better or worse, they create a world and a way of understanding ourselves which we internalize as our home reality.

Whatever else Christianity is about, it involves the shaping of the fundamental layers of our identities – our home realities. It is about seeing ourselves as God sees us. It is about being open to the perception that we are profoundly loveable and loved. Converting to Christianity is not a surface changing of beliefs and behaviours. It is a thoroughgoing process of reunderstanding who we are. This may be a slow process of identification which begins in childhood or it may be initiated quite suddenly later in life. In either case, if the process of conversion is not to be superficial, profound emotional attachments will be made as the person's home reality is shaped.

The purpose of Christian mission is to help others trust the God who identifies with them in Jesus Christ.

The approach of St Paul suggests that the purpose of Christian mission is to help others to trust the God who identifies with them in Christ, rather than trying to make others think and behave like we do. In seeking to introduce others to Christ we hold on to the conviction that it is safe to allow God power in human lives precisely because God is not looking for clones of himself in the way that human beings so often unwittingly turn out to be doing. God is not a cynical or insecure human being trying to shape our lives. God is the source of our being and our heart's desire. God, in Christ has already made a pilgrimage into the heart of our existence.

The implication for mission of God's pilgrimage into our humanity is that God is already present in each human life. Each embodied existence is already a mask of God. To encourage one another to make a journey deeper into our own humanity is to lead one another deeper into the place where the Spirit of Christ may be found. To present to one another images and pictures and stories of Christ which have connected us with profound aspects of our experience helps us to recognize that the Christ who comes to meet us on the road is one with the Spirit within us. In this light mission is about joining people on the journeys of their lives; making space for their stories and issues and deepest questions in the manner of Christ on the way to Emmaus. Mission becomes sharing with those whom we meet our profound sense of kinship with God in Christ through the stories and images and experiences that have brought it home to us. Mission becomes our continued pilgrimage with others into the living heart of the God who has made all of humanity his home.

Day 1
Christ comes to meet us on the road

Now on that same day two of them were going to a village called Emmaus, about seven miles from Jerusalem, and talking with each other about all these things that had happened. While they were talking and discussing, Jesus himself came near and went with them.

Luke 24.13–15

Image used with the permission of the Abádia de Santo Domingo de Silos.

In Jesus of Nazareth, God makes a pilgrimage to earth, committing himself to journey with people, patiently waiting for the moment when they can recognize him as the source of all that is good.

As in this eleventh-century depiction of Christ on the road to Emmaus, often our eyes are kept from recognizing him. It is too incredible to believe that the God who created the heavens and the earth seeks us out and longs to see our face. Blinded by disappointment or grief, like these disciples, we can find ourselves stumbling along, without hope.

Yet in the Emmaus story is Christ's purpose in miniature. He seeks us out, even as we walk in the wrong direction, accompanying us, listening to us and helping us to understand that to follow him is the path to life.

In many traditions life is conceived as a journey or a road. Sometimes the road is pleasing to walk and the path straightforward. Sometimes the road is difficult and we are pausing continually, looking for landmarks or guides to help us find our way. At other times we can be so consumed by our own feelings that we are blind even to the signposts that are there. Life seems to be going nowhere and we stumble along because there is no choice but to keep moving.

 How would you describe the road that you are travelling at the moment?

The disciples on the road to Emmaus were walking away from Jerusalem. They were despondent. They were consumed with their own disappointment and loss. They were blind to the presence of Christ alongside them.

 Looking back over your life, have there been times when Christ has been walking with you, but you were unaware of it?

 In what guises has Christ come to you?

 How have you come to recognize him?

Christ our companion,
you walk with us on the journey of our life;
you accompany us even as we are walking away;
you stand with us in our confusion
and refuse to let us go.
Open our eyes to your presence
and our hearts to your good news.
Guide our feet in the ways that lead to life.
Amen.

Day 2

I am the Resurrection and the Life

'Oh, how foolish you are, and how slow of heart to believe all that the prophets have declared! Was it not necessary that the Messiah should suffer these things and then enter into his glory?' Then beginning with Moses and the prophets, he interpreted to them the things about himself in all the scriptures.

Luke 24.25–27

This pilgrim has had enough. Like the disciples on the road to Emmaus she has lost hope and meaning. Like them she has heard rumours of resurrection, but at this moment they make no sense. Like them she knows the scriptures, yet they do not seem relevant or powerful here. What is real is her own exhaustion and the distance still to be travelled before dark. All she longs for is comfort and companionship on the journey she must make, with no thought for its direction.

When life overwhelms us, it is easy for us to pray for comfort and companionship alone, yet although, as in the Emmaus story Christ will come to meet us and patiently walk with us wherever we are going, a meeting with Christ does not necessarily confirm us in the direction our lives were taking. Encountering Christ introduces us to a more excellent way of life which he has already entered.

- Draw the life of Christ as a journey with resurrection life as its destination.

- Now draw your own life as a road. Think about where you have come from and where you are headed.

- How do the two roads you have drawn relate to each other?

For some people there are dramatic moments of conversion in their lives, when life takes a new and radical turn. Others feel they have always been on the road of discipleship. Yet, whether we have had a sudden conversion experience or not, the Christian life is an ongoing process of conversion in which Christ is calling us to turn from all that is destructive and life-draining towards that which gives life.

- Think about your life at the moment. What is draining you of life?

- Ask Christ to lead you deeper into his resurrection life.

Pilgrim God,
we long for you to come and meet us where we are,
but we are not always ready for our lives to change direction.
As we come to realize the depth of your love for us
help us to trust the paths in which you lead us.
Give us courage to abandon the wastelands in which we have wandered
and choose again the pilgrim way. Amen.

Day 3

Veiled in flesh the Godhead see!

In the beginning was the Word, and the Word was with God, and the Word was God. And the Word became flesh and lived among us, and we have seen his glory, the glory as of a father's only son, full of grace and truth. No one has ever seen God. It is God the only Son, who is close to the Father's heart, who has made him known.

John 1.1,14,18

Image © Pheoris West. Used with permission

The power in this image of Christ, like others that concentrate upon Christ's humanity, is the opportunity it presents for identification with him. Because the Christ here is so evidently human he is recognizable to us. The mystery that is hinted at by the presence of the dove and the movement in the picture is that he is also fully God. Only one who is fully God is able to demonstrate in his person that humanity essentially belongs to God and is fulfilled when it is one with him. In Christian prayers and songs it is difficult to hold together the two natures of Christ in one person, and yet when we are able to do so, the meaning of Emmanuel, God with us, is made clear. It is not just that an inspirational human leader appears on earth, but God's very self. As Charles Wesley says in one of his Christmas hymns: 'Being's source begins to be and God himself is born'.

Pictures of Christ as a black person or in contemporary dress may seem to us to be anachronistic. Rarely, however, have depictions of Jesus attempted historical accuracy. Many of the most famous images in western art have presented him as white and western and dressed, not as a first-century Palestinian, but in the clothes of the society that commissioned the painting. Such conventions may be read as an attempt by western civilization to colonize Christ, and yet when Jesus is depicted in the guise of those who have been discriminated against, a different message is portrayed – a message of Christ's identification with the whole human race.

 What images of Jesus help you to recognize both God and yourself in him?

 What Christmas carol best expresses for you the mystery of the incarnation?

 Read or sing it through for yourself as a prayer.

God's identification with the human race is most explicitly celebrated at Christmas. Charles Wesley expresses this extraordinary news in his hymn, 'Glory be to God on high':

God the invisible appears:
    God, the blest, the great I AM,
Sojourns in this vale of tears,
    And Jesus is his name.

Knees and hearts to him we bow;
    Of our flesh and of our bone,
Jesus is our brother now,
    And God is all our own.[10]

Day 4
The naked pilgrim

He was despised and rejected by others; a man of suffering and acquainted with infirmity; and as one from whom others hide their faces, he was despised, and we held him of no account. Surely he has borne our infirmities and carried our diseases; yet we accounted him stricken, struck down by God and afflicted. But he was wounded for our transgressions, crushed for our iniquities; upon him was the punishment that made us whole, and by his bruises we are healed.

Isaiah 53.3–5

Our visions of holiness are often pictures of light and purity; our images of Christ of beauty and all the fullness of God. We long to escape from the messiness of human life; we wish we could get away from painful memories; we want to rise above all that keeps us depressingly human. The temptation is to believe that we can simply bury all that we want to leave behind and rise above it. This image of the naked pilgrim, scarred by leprosy, and this passage from Isaiah remind us that in becoming human, Christ identifies with the ugliest and most painful parts of human life. In taking on human flesh Christ demonstrates that holiness comes not from ignoring the mess of the human condition, but through entering more deeply into it. Although this is a painful and difficult journey the incarnate God is there ahead of us. It is he who has carved out the way.

It is a common human reaction to recoil from suffering, disease and deformity. Perhaps it is from fear of infection, or from fear that these things too might befall us – things which are too awful to contemplate and are best kept out of sight and out of mind. Although passages like this one from Isaiah are applied to Christ most of the time when we depict Jesus – even on the cross – it is a romanticized picture we paint. Even in suffering the body of Jesus is often represented as the body beautiful.

 What instinctive reactions do you have to sufffering, disease and deformity?

 How do you react to the naked pilgrim as an image of Jesus?

Suffering, disease and deformity are rarely romantic, but Jesus is clear. He is to be found not among the beautiful people whose humanity is polished and airbrushed for display. Rather he is to be found among the sick and the imprisoned, the homeless and the naked and those in genuine need.

Just as Christ is to be found among those the world most despises, so he seeks to encounter us in the ugliest and most unbearable aspects of our lives. Allowing Christ to embrace what we find most difficult to accept in ourselves opens us to encountering him in those from whom we might otherwise recoil.

Lord Jesus Christ, in your body
you turned the values of the world inside out:
when we admired beauty – you showed us goodness;
when we sought refuge – you showed us sacrifice;
when we longed for innocence – you offered us redemption.
Lord Jesus Christ, as your body in the world,
turn our values upside down,
that we may find and serve you with joy.
Amen.

Day 5
As the Father sent me, so I send you

When it was evening on that day, the first day of the week, and the doors of the house where the disciples had met were locked for fear of the Jews, Jesus came and stood among them and said, 'Peace be with you.' After he said this, he showed them his hands and his side. Then the disciples rejoiced when they saw the Lord. Jesus said to them again, 'Peace be with you. As the Father has sent me, so I send you.'

John 20.19-21

Image used with the permission of the Abádia de Santo Domingo de Silos.

Christ is God's mission to the world. He is the pattern of any authentic reaching out to others in the name of God. The whole life of the incarnate Christ, depicted here in his encounter with doubting Thomas from Silos, speaks of God's patient willingness to sojourn with the human race – even at great cost to himself – still bearing the scars of torture and death, he offers even his wounds to Thomas in order to help him understand the way to life.

As Christ was sent by the Father, so we are sent in mission. Any authentic mission or ministry in the name of Jesus Christ requires a patient willingness to sojourn with people, even at cost to ourselves. It is motivated by the same love that brings the Word to birth.

Yet sometimes our efforts in mission can be overtaken by the desire to preserve ourselves or can turn into debates about styles of worship. Although finding an appropriate language in which to communicate is important, mission can never be reduced to less than love. Mission which convinces never costs less than our whole selves engaged in journeying with others.

 Think of a time when someone has had the patience and commitment to make a difficult journey with you, how was their commitment reflective of the love of God?

 Think about those amongst whom you live and work. Who is God calling you to walk alongside? What kind of commitment might this mean?

Gracious God,
in Christ you are patient with us,
committing yourself to flesh and blood
that we might recognize and trust you
as the source of our life.
Give us patience and courage
to love others with the same costly commitment,
prepared to travel with them
through the worst that life can do
until together we can rejoice in your presence
and delight in your love.
Amen.

75

Day 6
Treasure in clay jars

But we have this treasure in clay jars, so that it may be made clear that this extraordinary power belongs to God and does not come from us. We are afflicted in every way but not crushed; perplexed but not driven to despair; persecuted, but not forsaken; struck down, but not destroyed; always carrying in the body the death of Jesus, so that the life of Jesus may also be made visible in our bodies.

2 Corinthians 4.7–11

Boots caked in red mud sit outside this pilgrim hostel in Belorado in the heart of La Rioja, reminding pilgrims of their humanity. We are made from the same carbons and minerals as the rest of creation. We are as brittle as clay jars. Yet our vulnerability as human beings is not a flaw, but opens us to the possibility of encounter with others and with God.

Within us is planted the image of God. A journey into our own humanity will open up the treasure within, allowing the life of Christ to shine through. Denying our mortality and our frailty and fallibility keeps the treasure locked in. It makes us seem self-righteous and hypocritical and self-deceiving. Owning up to being openly broken people allows Christ to be seen at work, healing and forgiving and making whole.

 Think of a time when you have received ministry from someone else in their weakness.

It perhaps seems ironic that it is not always our best efforts that speak to others of the grace and forgiveness of God, but the evidence that we are human beings with feet of clay, who have yet learned that we are forgiven and are in need of a wholeness which we cannot attain for ourselves.

The ministry of the body of Christ is not only about what we actively set out to achieve, but what we endure. It is not only about the skills and techniques we learn for communication, but about our willingness to welcome people into our homes and our lives as fellow human beings, together seeking redemption.

 How well are you willing to be known in order to communicate God's grace?

 What is it about you that you would rather God did not need to use?

All-seeing and all-forgiving God,
that which we hide from ourselves
we think we have successfully concealed from those around us.
Little do we suspect that it is the cracks in our armour
that might allow your grace to shine through.
Grant us honesty with ourselves
and a sense of proportion,
that we may grow in grace
and in the service of others.
Amen.

4: Strangers and Pilgrims
– from Burgos to Astorga

This contemporary image of medieval pilgrims helping each other along the way is painted on a church wall in Sarria

From Burgos to Astorga

The road out of the city of Burgos was a lonely one. Once the yellow arrows have wound around the cathedral, the pilgrim path heads out towards the most notoriously deserted and monotonous part of the Camino, the plains of Castille. When I first thought of making this pilgrimage, I knew that the parts I would walk alone would be the most

Walking across the plains of Castille was my first experience of feeling really alone.

challenging. I had structured the trip so that in the first fortnight I was in the company of friends from home. As the time came for them to depart, the prospect of being alone on this road for a month was a daunting one. I stood on the high ground of the castle in Burgos and looked down on the cathedral spires. I looked eastwards, back over the way I had come – the way I knew – and thought about the friends who had accompanied me to this point. And then I turned to the west and looked at the yellow road snaking out through the medieval streets into the unknown.

The weather was cold and the wind biting as I battled my way out of the town and followed the line of the railway through reeds and then over the river. At first I felt intrepid, striking out on my own, but by evening I was glad to stop at the restored medieval hospital at Rabé del Camino: a square house filled with pilgrim artefacts, offering a meal at a common table and a massage for tired feet. Yet although the welcome was warm, the house was cold, the four other pilgrims spoke only French. French was therefore the language of the evening meal, and although I could follow some of the conversation, tired and cold, my concentration was not good enough to let me compose sentences in a language I have barely used since leaving school. It was my first experience of feeling really alone.

But this was only the beginning. The morning dawned colder and wet, and hauling myself up onto the plains I could not believe the force of the wind. Eyes squinting against the storm and the driving hailstones, I had to bend my head against my chest in order to breathe. Progress was slow and felt even slower – the landscape, lacking landmarks, just didn't seem to move. I had intended to walk well into the afternoon in order to reach the Knights Templar town of Castrojeriz, but the wind forced me off the track at the first opportunity. I headed towards a tiny cluster of buildings known as Arroyo Sanbol. The guidebook indicates that this place had once been a leper colony and at another time the home of a Jewish community, fleeing persecution. Its remoteness certainly spoke to me of exile. Although I had hoped to find the small hostel open, there was no sign of life: the extent of the hospitality on offer was a wall to shelter behind and a row of trees to break up the relentless wind. Breathlessly I sat down and pulled out my emergency rations to try to recoup some strength.

I found myself sitting looking at a spring. Pilgrims who bathe in it are said to have no more trouble with their feet until they reach Santiago. Suffering with blisters, as usual, despite the freezing cold, I unlaced my boots and bathed my feet, wondering about the generations of pilgrims who have done this – and how many of them believed that the miracle would work – and how many were simply grateful to reach a community here, high upon these inhospitable plains. I wondered how long it would be before I met someone who could speak to me in my own language; how long it would be before I would be warm again; how long I would have to manage alone.

Having eaten everything I had with me I reluctantly began to lace up my boots. I had no real energy to move on, but knew that staying here on my own, getting colder and stiff would not get me to a bed for the night. As I stood up, two figures appeared over the wall. It is difficult to describe how grateful I was to see them: two strangers dressed in black and orange, who greeted me in Spanish – the language of the Camino – and then lapsed into sign language as I had no German, and they, no English. We smiled at each other in sheer relief at meeting other human life. I helped them off with their rucksacks and we laughed together as they washed their feet in the spring. When I made signs that I needed to move on, they handed me a survival bar of fruit and nuts, to help me on my way.

This small act of kindness remained with me for days after our meeting and long after I had eaten the last of the food. The trek across the plains continued to be demanding and the hostels cold; my fellow pilgrims were mostly a large group of French who were travelling together and spoke too fast and furiously for me to join in; I was lonely and, at times, miserable, and yet the hospitality of this couple towards me, a complete stranger, was sustaining.

Becoming the stranger

The experience of walking across the plains was a glimpse into the vulnerable world of being the stranger. I was aware of my physical vulnerability as a single woman walking alone. I was aware of my emotional isolation, able to communicate basic needs in Spanish and French but unable to tell anyone how I was feeling. I was dependent upon the willingness of those with greater resources than I to enter into my experience, to listen to my body language and to take the imaginative leap of putting themselves in my shoes.

The experience of being the stranger is an essential part of the pilgrim story.

It was an insecure place to be, dependent upon the imagination and good will of others and I began to think about life from the perspective of the stranger – the refugee, the asylum seeker, the homeless person, the person living outside the familiar surroundings of their racial and cultural background. I began to notice that others travelling on their own or in pairs, who were also susceptible to the same isolation as I was, were much more tuned in to my presence and made much more effort to include me, despite language barriers, than those travelling in established groups.

The experience of being a stranger is an essential part of the pilgrim story. Given how strangers are often treated in the world around us this is a daunting prospect. Knowing how easy it is to feel threatened by strangers and to fear their intentions towards us, particularly if they look different

What experience do you have of being a stranger? How did it feel?

from us by virtue of being from another faith tradition, race or culture, becoming a stranger gives the pilgrim a new perspective on the world. For those of us used to being surrounded by family and friends and having status and roles to help us know who we are and how to be, the Camino is the way of dispossession: in a new culture where even one's own language is of limited use, identity is stripped of many of its layers. Occupation, education, appearance and family roles are of little consequence here. The pilgrim relies on the ability of others to perceive their humanity and to be compassionate.

For me it was a salutary experience. It was a shock to be ignored or to be treated as of little account. As a minister I am used to being at the centre of things. Even when moving to new places or visiting churches for the first time, I am used to being welcomed and given a place in the community by virtue of my role. But even as I have been welcomed into village life and into the life of churches as one who belongs, I have been aware that the experience of others who have tried to join in without such status, has been different. The attention of existing communities has often been upon its existing members and newcomers have been politely, albeit unintentionally, left out of the loop.

I know this is true in the community in which I live and work. Although Methodists and Jews and Orthodox Christians all live on the same site and are on nodding terms with one another it takes deliberate effort and initiative to make real relationships with those outside the circle of one's own pressing concern. When you are on the inside it is easy to focus on the things the existing group shares, speaking the private language of acronyms and structures that are essential to the smooth running of an organization but are as impenetrable as a foreign language to those on the outside. The stranger is left to wonder what it is all about.

Here, on these plains, my experience of being on the outside focused my attention in a different direction. Because I was aware of my own basic needs for food and human contact, I could feel a common humanity with those people from whom I was different. Yet to them, already belonging to a group, I seemed strange, irrelevant and perhaps a threat to their established ways of relating and seeing the world. I began to see the parable of the Good Samaritan through the eyes of the vulnerable traveller who was mugged on the road. I began to realize that hospitality arises from seeing the world from the traveller's point of view.

Hospitality to pilgrims

Such an ethic of hospitality is at the heart of the traditions of the Camino. Indeed, the journey is only possible because of the hostels that welcome pilgrims along the way. Although some are now municipal foundations which are run on quite impersonal lines, many are still run by religious communities or by former pilgrims and dedicated individuals whose lives are committed to welcoming the stranger.

At the monastery at Roncesvalles on the Spanish side of the Pyrenees there is a tradition of hospitality unbroken since the tenth century. It is summed up in a thirteenth-century poem:

The gate is open to everyone:
to the sick and to the well;
not only to Catholics
but also to unbelievers,
to Jews, heretics
and vagabonds as well.

The ethic of the pilgrimage is to offer hospitality to any who come, regardless of religious affiliation or background.

Initially it had come as a surprise to me that many of those who travel the pilgrim road to Santiago do not count themselves Catholic or even Christian. It was an even greater surprise to learn that since their foundation, the monastic communities along the way, which have provided food and lodging and medical treatment to pilgrims for generations, have always done so regardless of the religious tradition to which their guests belonged.

The welcome takes a variety of forms. At Roncesvalles the hospitality was formal and the invitation was to receive a blessing for the journey. Most of the pilgrims, whether they were believers or not, came to the Mass and, at the end, came forward to be blessed in the traditional words.

In other places the welcome is different though no less sincere. In San Juan de Ortega it takes the form of garlic soup made by an ancient monk. It is available free of charge to any who dare. In the church tower at Grañon, the priest listens to pilgrims and shares his meal with them; invites them to pray in their own language and encourages them to use the box for donations which is labelled, 'Give if you can; take if you need'. As I walked across the plains I met an Austrian woman who told me she had never really thought about Christianity before but who had been deeply impressed by the priest at Grañon, by his honesty and his willingness to share himself, and by his humility as he listened to pilgrims at night and hung off the bell tower by day to repair the church roof.

But whatever form the welcome takes it is offered to anyone who wants to travel the route, whether they are religious or not. Along the way I met many people travelling for personal or loosely spiritual reasons whose roots were not Christian, and others who were simply interested in an ancient path. One evening I ate with a Japanese man who knew nothing about the route before he set out, except that a friend in America had told him there were hostels across northern Spain that would enable him to walk from the Pyrenees to the coast. On another occasion I shared a picnic with a Dutch man who had lost his wife; of no religious faith himself, he thought the walking would give him time and space to mourn. A young man from Germany told me in a bar one night that someone from each generation of his family had walked the Camino going back five generations. He had decided that he would maintain the tradition and make the trip as a way of deciding whether to make a major career change.

People walk for a whole host of reasons, and many of them are managing the major life-changes of bereavement and retirement or divorce or looking for new direction in life. I had anticipated that on a Catholic pilgrimage I would spend a good deal of time with people of faith. Although I did meet Christians, both pilgrims and those offering hospitality, in fact, the Camino is an international meeting ground for people of very different backgrounds and world-views, all of whom, though strangers and sometimes strange, are fellow pilgrims and according to the Camino's ethic of hospitality are to be treated with generosity and respect.

The ethic is enacted in small ways. At each hostel there is a table or shelf on which pilgrims are invited to leave gifts for other pilgrims. All sorts of things accumulate and are available to anyone who needs them. One pilgrim might leave the remains of a loaf of bread they do not need; another a redundant pair of shoes. As people begin to take the ethos to heart, they buy more

Have you ever been genuinely dependent upon the kindness of strangers?

plasters or sun cream or fruit than they need in order to leave some for others whose financial resources are more strained.

The tradition harks back to a time when pilgrims were forbidden to take money with them on the journey. Stripped of the power and status that comes with money and the ability to invite others into their own sphere of influence, the pilgrim was to learn to be a guest. Today, most pilgrims do carry money, although their means vary enormously. Official hostels, however, maintain the tradition of donations. Even if a fixed amount is suggested it is not demanded from those without means. Local people also maintain traditions of hospitality to pilgrims. Boxes of apples will be left by the wayside marked, 'para pelegrinos'; the vinegrowers of La Rioja offer cups of wine, and at Irache in Navarre, the vineyard has a wine fountain installed, although over indulging is not recommended when there is a long way to walk in the sun.

At one level these gifts are a quaint and nostalgic reminder of days gone by. At another level, there are times when the pilgrim, far from home, is still genuinely dependent upon the kindness of another to point them back on the path when they are lost, or to get them to a clinic when they cannot walk. Such experiences remind the pilgrim of the truth that none of us is an island. At home, surrounded by one's own possessions and circle of family and friends, this fact of life can be obscured. In a strange country, trying to make oneself understood in a strange language, the pilgrim soon becomes aware of their need of the friendship and the care of others. The experience is an invitation into a different way of life.

Hospitality: a biblical way of life

Hospitality as a way of life is deeply embedded in the culture of the Bible. This is well illustrated by the story of the visitation to Abraham and Sarah. In Genesis 11, Abraham and Sarah, who are themselves strangers in the land, receive three unknown guests at their tent in the wilderness.

Although the visitors are strangers and arrive unexpectedly, Abraham and Sarah feel an obligation to them as fellow travellers in the desert. Doubtless knowing what it is to be dependent on the hospitality of others themselves, they not only provide the minimal bread and water and shade that Abraham originally offers, but bring out curds and milk and the calf prepared, presumably, for another occasion. In one sense this story reflects a culture very different from that which prevails in the western world and it would have been more remarkable if Abraham and Sarah had treated the strangers differently. And yet, the point of the biblical story is not simply to commend an ethic of hospitality as being of mutual benefit in society. The story is about encounter with God, for it is in welcoming the unexpected guest that God is made known. As the letter to the Hebrews puts it, 'Do not neglect to show hospitality to strangers, for by doing that some have entertained angels without knowing it' (Hebrews 13.2).

According to the Bible, it is in welcoming the unexpected guest that God is made known.

The story is presented, not merely as an encounter between three strangers and the old couple, but as an encounter with God. After one of the strangers has promised Sarah a son, Abraham, according to the custom, sets the strangers on their way. But it is the Lord's voice he hears as he travels with them.

Here is a story from scriptures that Muslims and Christians and Jews hold in common which grounds the practice of hospitality to strangers as a holy way of life which may open us to the presence of God. In a world in which tensions between people of different faith are rising, perhaps it is an ethic of hospitality and a sense of people of other faiths as fellow pilgrims that are needed in interfaith relations today. This is an ethic which goes way beyond the tolerance advocated by governments and invites the stranger, even the potential enemy, into the heart of one's own home. It involves risk and generosity and openness to learning through friendship with those who are different from us.

As such, the practice of hospitality not only opens us to an encounter in which God may be revealed, but reflects the very nature of God's self. In Christian thought, the story of the visitation to Abraham has been thought to reveal God's very being as one of gracious hospitality. Picking up on the fact that the visitors in the story are sometimes three separate individuals and sometimes one who speaks as the Lord, the three figures have been interpreted as the three persons of the Trinity: Father, Son and Holy Spirit. The ambiguity in the story is famously represented by Rublev in his icon of the Visitation to Abraham (see page 94). Here, the three figures are seated at the table. They are the visitors to Abraham; they are angelic messengers with wings; they are God: Father, Son and Holy Spirit, inviting us into communion with them.

Gracious hospitality is at the heart of God's very being.

God's very self, in this image of the Trinity, is presented as community. The three persons look attentively at each other, illustrating the constant dynamic which Christians believe is at the heart of God. But the community is not a closed community. Rather, the fourth side of the table is open as an invitation to anyone who would gaze into the picture and be drawn into the communion of God's love. In Rublev's interpretation of the Genesis story the roles are reversed. Ostensibly the story is about Abraham's generosity to three strangers. But as Abraham makes room for them at his table and in the conversation he, and we, are drawn into the life of God, where we are the ones who receive.

Christians are charged to welcome the stranger by remembering that we, too, are guests, dependent on the generous hospitality of God.

This interpretation of the story turns hospitality on its head. For Christians, the fundamental reality of our life is that we are guests within God's hospitality. If we have homes and means, these are not ours by right to do with what we please, but are ours to steward for the sake of the whole of humanity which God loves. The people of Israel were charged to welcome the stranger by remembering that they had been strangers in Egypt. Christians are charged to welcome the stranger by remembering that we, too, are guests, dependent on the generous hospitality of God.

Practising hospitality towards those who are different from us is a counter-intuitive way to live. It challenges the view of many religious people that contact between people of different faiths should only be for the sake of conversion and it challenges the natural tendency of human beings to stick to what we know and to find safety with those who are like us and who reinforce our ways of seeing the world. Yet those who worship the God whose nature is generous hospitality cannot help but be drawn into a way of being that is open to the stranger.

Turning towards the stranger

The contrast between human attitudes towards hospitality and God's generosity can be demonstrated by looking at two accounts of meals in the life of Jesus. In the first story Jesus is a guest at the house of Simon the Pharisee (Luke 7.36–50). He goes to eat with Simon, but Simon does not extend to him the basic courtesies of the culture: he does not kiss him in greeting; he does not offer water in order to bathe his feet. All this comes to light when Simon is outraged that a woman who is a notorious sinner is found pouring out perfume and tears at Jesus' feet.

Simon's lack of hospitality raises the question of why Simon had invited Jesus in the first place – perhaps as an entertainment for his respectable friends. In a collection of sayings related later in the Gospel of Luke, Jesus has plenty to say about only inviting to banquets those who will repay you by inviting you in return. (Luke 14:12-14). He is scathing about the culture of hospitality which does nothing but display the wealth and status of the host and pays scant attention to the needs of the guests.

What motivates the hospitality you offer in your own home?

By contrast, at the Last Supper, it is Jesus himself who takes off his outer garment, kneels on the floor and attends to the needs of his guests. Hospitality which is worthy of the name makes genuine space for others, is not worried about status or control and attends to the actual needs of those it seeks to serve. It thinks about the world from the perspective of the stranger, from the perspective of the one in need.

Hospitality which is worthy of the name makes genuine space for others and thinks about the world from the perspective of the stranger.

What is highlighted in Jesus' stories about banquets is the all-too-human tendency to make common cause with those we find conducive company to the exclusion of those who are different from us. This is community based on our own interests and on our own fears and neediness. Whatever our rhetoric, often what we really want is to find others with whom we can band together so that the world is not so frightening; we want to find people like us who understand us and see the world in the ways that we do. When we have established alliances and feel secure we will invest a large amount of energy in suppressing the ways that we are different in order to maintain our common interests.

Even on the Camino, where openness to the stranger is encouraged, I was painfully reminded of my own tendency to look for like-minded, or even just familiar, people. Although at times I congratulated myself that I had come on this pilgrimage alone and was open to new encounters, in practice I tended to find easy travelling companions and stick with them. The surprise was that each time I was forced to part company with a familiar companion, before too long there were new people to greet. Whenever I gave up looking for those who would be conducive company and opened myself to the people who happened to be there, the experience was qualitatively different.

Although the first few days up on the plains of Castille without my companions were lonely, I did begin to pay more attention to the strangers that I met. This was partly out of relief at finding other human life, but it was also because I was beginning to be able to welcome the stranger within myself.

Welcoming the stranger within

It is a paradox that only those who can bear solitude are ready for community, while only those who can bear community are ready for solitude. Learning to bear a little more of my own company high on those plains, I began to realize that sometimes I seek company in order to avoid myself.

'Each one makes their own Camino' is a phrase often heard on the road in a variety of languages. It is one of the wisdoms of the pilgrimage. It means that pilgrims need to listen to their own needs; to the still small voice within them, and to walk at their own pace; to stop when it feels right without being too bound to someone else's timetable. I found it a real challenge to try to do this. Instead of making space to listen to the voice of unconditional love out of which I might greet others, another instinct, deeply rooted, wanted to find allies, people to be with so that the rawness of my own vulnerability would be masked.

Genuine hospitality comes not from an avoidance of our own loneliness, but an embracing of the stranger within ourselves.

The result was that on one occasion I walked on for three days past my rest day in order to keep up with a group I had fallen in with. With each day my feet became more painful. Finally the soles erupted all over with tiny blisters – all of this because I wouldn't listen to the small voice within me that was begging me to stop. Booking into a guest-house, at first I was anxious and disappointed, realizing that I would not see my friends again – they would get to Santiago before me – but then, as I realized that my feet were really quite bad, I began to berate myself for trying to keep up with someone else's pace – and for what? Simply for fear of being left alone. To make matters worse, I now had to ask for help. The response to my request was so kind that I was reduced to tears. I could not be kind to the stranger within myself – this voice that I did not want to hear – but this stranger could be.

As I began to realize my tendency to seek the comforting companionship of people like me on pilgrimage, so equally I began to recognize the ways in which I have sought allies within the Church who would agree with me before I opened my mouth, rather than opening myself to encounter with those I might find strange. Moreover, it seemed that so often what I had thought was Christian fellowship was little more than like-minded people enjoying each other's company, sometimes as protection from the truth that there are essential ways in which we are, and need to be, alone.

Breaking company with friends for a while when the relationship has become insular and based on fear of the alternatives rather than upon truth does not absolve us from responsibility towards our friends. It may help us, though, to hear again the voice of love which is not only our salvation but theirs. It is this knowledge of ourselves as beloved of God which opens to Christians the possibility of rejecting the false comfort of communities based upon seeking out people who are like us, or which are centred around the powerful who can offer us their protection. Community founded in the love of God requires of us nothing but receiving within us the truth that we belong together, as sinners. None of us earned the right to be here. None of us need earn it. All of us belong because, unaccountably, we are loved by God. Receiving this love and living out of it is the only thing that will enable us not to band together for our own justification, but to embrace those who are different from us. None of us need curry favour, or seek admiration, or build a power base, for we already belong; we are justified by grace. We need only learn to trust it.

87

The fruit of trusting is sometimes greater than we can imagine. Sitting outside the guest-house, enjoying some of the first real sunshine since I'd left the French side of the Pyrenees, I was delighted to see two former walking companions pulling their way up the slope to join me. In truth, though I recognized them, I had not previously had much to do with them. Last time I had seen them I already had an established group of people to walk with, yet although I was now alone I was no longer looking for others to hold together my identity. I was ready to welcome whoever had come up the hill as genuine others with their own needs, needing to walk at their own pace.

Responding to the heat pouring off them I pulled out two chairs and went in search of cold drinks. We exchanged tales of what had happened to us since we last met, and, before long they were ready to move on. Still grounded by the doctor and needing to rest my feet I watched them continue up the hill. I hoped I would see them again, but although the encounter had been brief, it had been real, and I felt that at this little table at the side of the road I had entertained angels unawares.

Part of what had helped me to find myself again as someone able to offer genuine hospitality without strings attached was acknowledging my own need and allowing myself to hear the voice of the stranger within me. Receiving help at the hands of others reminded me that I am held and loved and need not be anxious; that what I need to remember to do is trust.

One of the most potent reminders for Christians that we are held in being by the hospitality of God is the celebration of Holy Communion. Communicants are invited to come and kneel and be fed, not because they have any right to do so, but because they know their need. To participate in this feast is not simply to eat with friends or strangers, but it is to commune with God in Christ, receiving a foretaste of the heavenly banquet prepared for all people. For those who belong Communion can be a potent experience of God's overwhelming desire to welcome us to the feast of the kingdom; certainly it was sustaining for me regularly to receive the bread and wine as I travelled, yet in the company of those unaccustomed to christian worship I began to realize that communion can seem a strange and alienating rite, only accessible to those who are already 'holy'.

The Church as host

In the course of my pilgrimage across 500 miles I visited many churches. In some, the hospitality of God was profoundly enacted and I felt welcomed and loved. In many places, however, the stream of pilgrims passing through, with their questions and their searching and their need, seemed to make little impact upon the local Christian communities. Pilgrims were welcome at Mass, but there was little attempt to meet with them or help them to participate in the liturgy or make tangible the hospitality of God in any way. From the perspective of many pilgrims who would not normally even enter a church, to walk across the threshold was quite a step, to march right up to the altar was asking impossibly much.

The attitude which suggests that it is the responsibility of the Church to celebrate the banquet of God and expects the world to come and join in is one which is commonly found in churches. Perhaps, in the West, where the Church has been used to having power in society and being at the centre of debate about moral and social issues, this is not surprising, but it is also a symptom of the persistent human failure to grasp the radical nature of the basis of the hospitality that God offers.

When the Church remembers to trust in God's love, then we are drawn into welcoming people, whoever they are.

Christians, when we remember to trust in God's love for us as the basis of our security, are drawn into welcoming people whoever they are, seeking ways to enact for them and introduce them to the generous love of God by meeting their real needs. Wherever there is genuine Christian community, hospitality will be offered to the stranger, not as a display of the Church's power or status or as a way of maintaining the Church's image of itself at the centre of the wider community, but as a genuine making space for the other. This does not mean that we should not celebrate the hospitality of God in communion, but it does mean that it is the hospitality of God that we should be celebrating and by which we should be transformed.

The Benedictine nuns in León offered me a captivating example of such hospitality by inviting all the pilgrims who stay with them into the heart of their prayer life, each night, at Compline. Each night the bell is rung at 9.45 p.m. and one sister comes to collect the gathered pilgrims. Patiently, and using fragments of different languages, she welcomes the pilgrims and tries to introduce the liturgy to the motley selection of largely agnostic and unchurched, yet curious, visitors. This is done with humour and several rehearsals of the sung responses, and without any sense of demand. There is no expectation that pilgrims will return or contribute financially to the life of the house. There is no expectation that the pilgrims should know what to do. There is warmth and a genuine desire to meet others in their language and on their own journey and in their spiritual need, and to communicate with them their knowledge of God's yearning for relationship with all people.

My experience of the convent in León gave me courage to believe that it is possible for Christian communities to offer genuine welcome into the heart of their life when their life is founded upon God's generous hospitality towards humanity. Then, without coercion or manipulation, we are able to host well. Yet Christians in the West are very used to being the hosts. Hosting out of habit or a sense of prerogative can prevent us from really being responsive to the needs of our guests. Also, like other human beings, we also find it hard not to turn a community into an opportunity for furthering our own self-oriented interests: doing the comfortable things in the comfortable way meets our own needs rather than those we seek to serve, who have perhaps even stopped coming into our churches. Maybe the only way we can relearn genuine hospitality which is attentive to the real needs of others is to venture outside the walls of our churches and learn to enact God's hospitality as fellow guests at his table.

The Church as guest

This thought came to me at Villar de Mazarife, a short day's walk out of León. I arrived at the brand-new hostel in the mid-afternoon to be greeted by a young woman who introduced herself as Fabienna, the *hospitalera*. After a shower I sat on the lawn with a group of people all of whom were strangers to me: a Dutch couple; two French women travelling together; an Austrian; a Canadian; all of us going through the routines of pilgrims at the end of the day: treating blisters; massaging tired shoulders; writing our journals; drinking beer, taking small risks of kindness, of conversation.

On the door of the hostel a notice advertised that Fabienna would cook for us for 7 euros per head, but a scheme developed to cook all together. A trip to the village shop and a foray into the newly equipped kitchen produced a meal of pasta and salad and a table set with serviettes and candles. We had become a family with our hostess as guest. After the washing up and the coffee on the lawn in the fading light, Heidi, the Austrian, suggested a fire. And when we had made it, we sat around it, singing and laughing and then telling stories – at Fabienna's request, *real* stories of the Camino.

Heidi told the story of losing her guidebook – not once but several times between Burgos, where she began, and Léon. She took it as a sign that she was not ready to undergo the discipline of the Way but that day, on the way from Léon, she had found a stick at the side of the road that would make a staff. She knew it was hers, and found herself ready, some 200 km after she had set out, to begin.

Veronique, from Quebec, spoke of walking into a town between Burgos and León called Carrion de los Condes. Having already walked 25 km she looked for a hostel, but something inside was telling her to carry on and face the aloneness that was waiting. When she arrived in Calzada, some 17km further on, exhausted and starving, she knew she had faced something key in herself. Since then, she had not been afraid to be alone or to be with others.

Tristen, another Austrian, had been very quiet and protested that he had no story to tell, but in the respectful silence he confessed that he felt depleted, that he had lost direction, that he simply didn't know how to go on.

Fabienna, the *hospitalera*, told us how she had walked the Camino two years previously. She walked from the Pyrenees to Burgos with two friends but then knew she needed to be alone. The walk across the *meseta* was arduous and exhausting, yet she learned to be cared for by strangers and to trust to the next step of the journey. Back at home in Brazil she took a job in the theatre in Rio but having walked the Camino, she found she could no longer live on the rich side of the expanding poverty gap. She had come back to Spain to work as an *hospitalera* and to find her way to make a difference in the world.

I spoke about the nuns I had met in León, who had welcomed us to Compline, and whose unassuming Mother Superior had spoken to us in gentle tones about the purpose of pilgrimage: the need to walk in silence, the need to be attentive to one another, the importance of allowing space for the 'mysterious presence of Christ within us' to make himself known.

Into the silence that followed, Fabienna said she thought God was here, in both happiness and sadness. No one had professed a faith, but all were listening, intent on the fire, immersed in the moment and it seemed that naming God's presence was the most natural thing in the world. Then suddenly some local villagers appeared. As Tristen said, 'In my country if I saw travellers making a fire outside my house I would call the police!' but these elderly people wanted to join us, to bring us food, to talk about the Camino, to make us welcome.

The evening that I spent at Mazarife was a delightful evening which left a profound impact on me. When, smoky, in the small hours I left the fire and crawled into my sleeping bag I knew that here there was much food for thought. It is difficult to put into words, but here was a spontaneous and profound experience of human connection that I, and others, experienced as nothing less than holy.

Here I was challenged by a depth and honesty that I have not always found in church circles. Here, there was community rooted, not in a selfish banding together, but in a search for truth. Here were people who had faced their own needs and humanity and their own need of others and were no longer afraid of it. Here were people who did not need a false sense of community that relies on suppressing differences. Here was a community able to allow the other to be a person, in all their particularity. And here was a host who was able to make space for others and enact the hospitality of God even while being a guest.

What might it mean for the Church to become the guest?

Without the status of a priest or minister or the security of a convent or church project, Fabienna was able to allow herself to be our guest. Her ease, without the role and security that cooking for us could have offered her, was disarming. Whether intentionally or not, she allowed us to make her welcome in her own temporary home and so made the space for the group to be real, leading by example and inviting us to tell real stories of the Camino.

In this way, Fabienna was a sojourner herself, making fellow sojourners welcome. In learning to offer the hospitality of God from the place of the guest she was following in the steps of Jesus himself who, although he embodied the banquet of God in his very person, had no home of his own and was frequently a guest in the houses of the least likely of people.

As I moved on from Mazarife towards Astorga and the mountains beyond, it was the example of Fabienna that inspired me one evening to host a Communion service in the common room of the hostel where I was staying the night. After a morning tramping through the green and wet landscape of Galicia in the steaming rain I gave up the day's walk at a small dishevelled village called Eirexe. I was halted by the surreal sight of an ostrich in a garden and decided it was sufficiently bizarre a sign to stay the night. The hostel next door was deserted save for a small, wizened woman in her eighties who welcomed me in a high-pitched dialect and marched me off to watch her make cheese and introduce me to her dead relations in their tombs. She knelt in the church and wept and talked – something about Franco – and invited me to kiss the statue of St Lucia and bless my eyes.

Back at the hostel other pilgrims were arriving: two elderly Australian women; the two friends I had walked with, a French couple, a German, a Californian. As we gathered, the idea grew that we would like to celebrate Communion together. It seemed unlikely that our host would think her Catholic church an appropriate place for a grubby English woman to preside so – to her uncomprehending amazement – we set about transforming the common room of the hostel: a silk scarf for an altar cloth, bread and wine scrounged from the owners of the ostrich, who offered to cook us all a meal afterwards, a German psalter, a Spanish Gospel of Luke, Taizé chants in Latin, and at each point in the service, more pilgrims arrived, amazed to be invited to a 'mass' presided over by a woman and, even more to our surprise, everyone wanted to join in.

And as we shared the word together, each participant placing something of their own on the table: a map, a shell, a cross, a pressed flower, we heard each other's reasons for travelling: a retreat on the march, a bereavement, a holiday, a relationship break-up, a penance on behalf of a sick friend. And in our sharing – some of the stories and spiritualities familiar, some of them strange – there was a profound sense of the grace of God breaking through so that by the time we broke bread, as we offered the elements to one another, it seemed that Christ, both host and guest, was in our midst.

Perhaps the image of ourselves as guests who offer the hospitality of God is one that can help the churches of the West to focus beyond themselves. Once used to power and influence, we are finding ourselves more marginal in society and having to come to terms with the existence of communities with different values and loyalties from ours. In this context, perhaps the ethic of hospitality has something to offer. As Christians we tend to think that we are the ones called to offer hospitality in the name of God, and that conviction is summed

Perhaps it is art of being the guest that Christians in the West most need to recapture in the post-Christendom world.

up for us in the celebration of the Lord's Supper. The experience of pilgrimage, however, requires the pilgrim to become the stranger and learn to receive the hospitality of others.

This is a hard school of learning for those of us brought up within the Church. We are not used to articulating and explaining our beliefs, we are not used to starting where others want to begin, and we are not used to naming God in unfamiliar places. Perhaps it is the art of being the guest that Christians in the West most need to recapture in the post-Christendom world if we are to be experience holiness in encounter with those who are different from us and participate in the kind of community to which God is calling the whole of humanity.

Day 1
Receiving from God

Ho, everyone who thirsts,
come to the waters;
and you that have no money,
*   come, buy and eat!*
Come, buy wine and milk
without money and
*   without price.*

Isaiah 55.1

Rublev's icon of the three strangers' visitation to Abraham and Sarah represents God the Trinity. Father, Son and Holy Spirit are seated at three sides of a four-sided table. They are attentive to each other's gaze, visibly in communion with one another. On the table is placed a chalice of wine, a clear evocation of Holy Communion, that most significant of meals, in which we who look into the picture are invited to partake. God invites us into God's very life as we sit and eat at the fourth side of the table. We cannot earn our place; we have no role but to receive.

Receiving hospitality can be an uncomfortable experience for those used to being the hosts. For those used to cooking for a family, for example, it can be difficult to be without the defined role that being the host provides, or to believe that they are worthy of treatment as a guest. Others, more used to being cooked for, can expect to be served as their right. It scarcely occurs to them that hospitality is a gift to which they have no title. They have little joy in receiving.

Do you find it more uncomfortable to be the host or the guest?

Why do you think that is?

God invites us to receive with open hands. We have no entitlement to God's gift of himself in bread and wine; neither can we avoid receiving ourselves if we wish to be of service to others. Those who receive bread and wine become Christ's scattered body, given for the life of the world.

Open your hands in prayer to receive God's gifts to you.

Lord, I am not worthy to receive you,
but only say the word and I shall be healed.

Day 2
Becoming the stranger

He called the twelve and began to send them out two by two, and gave them authority over the unclean spirits. He ordered them to take nothing for their journey except a staff; no bread, no bag, no money in their belts; but to wear sandals and not to put on two tunics.

Mark 6.7–9

Some of the oldest monasteries along the Camino are Franciscan foundations. This is rumoured to be because St Francis himself made the pilgrimage to Santiago and was inspired by the Order of San Anton who provided hospitality for those suffering from St Anthony's fire, a particularly virulent form of leprosy.

St Francis required his monks to be permanent 'liminars'. They were always to live on the edge without resources of their own, dependent on the kindness of strangers, seeing the world from the perspective of Christ himself who had no place to lay his head, yet whose mission was to make others welcome. For St Francis there was virtue in being homeless and without possessions. Coming from a wealthy family himself, he felt called to divest himself of his material security in order to see life from the perspective of the stranger and so remember how to welcome others.

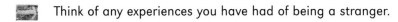 Think of any experiences you have had of being a stranger.

 What can they teach you about genuine hospitality?

It is difficult for those of us who live in the West in good living conditions with money for leisure and travel to imagine that words in the gospels about riches are to be taken seriously. Financial security is so fundamental to the way that we think as families and as churches that it is almost unthinkable to contemplate living as St Francis did. Moreover we live in an age when there is zero-tolerance of begging.

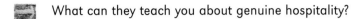 Why do you think Jesus sent out his disciples without money?

Lord Jesus,
found among the poorest and the least,
have mercy on us.

Christ Jesus,
found among the ill and the despised,
have mercy on us.

Lord Jesus,
found among the asylum seeker and the stranger,
teach us to seek your face.

Day 3
Give what you can, take what you need

All who believed were together and had all things in common; they would sell their possessions and goods and distribute the proceeds to all, as any had need. Day by day, as they spent much time together in the temple, they broke bread at home and ate their food with glad and generous hearts, praising God and having the goodwill of all the people. And day by day the Lord added to their number those who were being saved.

Acts 2.44–47

In the bell tower of the church in Grañon is a small hostel run by the priest and volunteers. Each night, prayers are said; pilgrims, whatever their beliefs, are encouraged to explore deep questions; a basic meal is provided and pilgrims invited to share their food; there is no charge. The donations box (below) reads: 'Give what you can, take what you need'.

Being a pilgrim establishes a link with other pilgrims even with those you never meet. Being a Christian is no different but how much are we ready to share, of our time, of our money, of our faith?

The ethos of the Early Church was not one of charity. It was one of sharing resources. These were not considered the private possession of one, but gifts to be shared for the building up of the kingdom and the relieving of need. It is perhaps easy to confine this kind of thinking to the New Testament, but in other generations Christians have tried to live by it. For example, John Wesley's first preachers lived in community at the Foundery in City Road, in London. They established a friendly society for themselves and for the provision of medicines for any who needed them. Those who received help from this fund were welcome to eat with them at their table.

The ethos of the Camino is similarly a long way from the kind of charity that does good to others from a great height or from a great distance. It seeks to build bonds between fellow pilgrims on the earth and a sense of shared responsibility for one another.

At the offering in church services it is common to pray, 'Lord, every good thing comes from you and of your own do we give you.'

 How do you view the money you earn or the earning power you have – to whom does it belong?

We ask God to bless the money we put in the collection plate, but what of the money and other resources that we retain?

 Are there changes you would like to make in the way you steward your money and material resources?

God, help us to change.
Let us be doers of your word
and not hearers only,
that your word in us may change the world.
Amen.

99

Day 4
Abraham welcomes strangers

The LORD appeared to Abraham by the oaks of Mamre, as he sat at the entrance of his tent in the heat of the day. He looked up and saw three men standing near him. When he saw them, he ran from the tent entrance to meet them, and bowed down to the ground. He said, 'My lord, if I find favour with you, do not pass by your servant. Let a little water be brought, and wash your feet and rest yourselves under the tree.'

Genesis 18.1-4

At his makeshift hostel, high in the mountains, Tomas (in the blue jacket) offers free coffee to passing pilgrims. The conditions in which Tomas lives are very basic and yet everyone is treated as a valued guest. Every time a pilgrim comes into view the bell is rung to welcome them.

 Think of a situation in which you sometimes feel ill at ease.

 How might you be the one to make others feel at home?

Abraham was a wanderer – a pilgrim who had set out on a journey of faith at the command of God. He had no fixed home, and yet he was willing to share the shade of the tree he had found in the heat of the day. When we are far from home or do not feel at home in ourselves or in our own neighbourhood, the human instinct is to retreat and conserve resources. Yet God is always inviting us to make room for the stranger, whether it is within our temporary home, in the queue in the doctor's waiting room or within a conversation. Hospitality involves listening, watching out for what the other person needs and making room for them to feel at home.

In the letter to the Hebrews, the writer tells the churches 'not to neglect hospitality for in so doing some have entertained angels unawares'. The reward of making room for others is that we ourselves are enlarged in the process. In welcoming the stranger, we become more like God's very self.

Generous God,
you opened your heart to be the host and welcome the stranger –
even stretched on a cross.
When we feel strange and estranged
and our resources are stretched to the limit,
give us grace to open our arms
and welcome those whom we fear
in the name of Love.
Amen.

Day 5
Who is my neighbour?

A man was going down from Jerusalem to Jericho, and fell into the hands of robbers, who stripped him, beat him, and went away, leaving him half dead. Now by chance a priest was going down that road; and when he saw him, he passed by on the other side. So likewise a Levite, when he came to the place and saw him, passed by on the other side. But a Samaritan while travelling came near him; and when he saw him, he was moved with pity. He went to him and bandaged his wounds, having poured oil and wine on them. Then he put him on his own animal, brought him to an inn, took out two denarii, gave them to the innkeeper, and said, 'Take care of him; and when I come back, I will repay you whatever more you spend.'

Luke 10.30–35

This fifteenth-century depiction of the Good Samaritan comes from the pilgrim hostel in Santiago.

Jesus told the parable of the Good Samaritan in answer to a question from a religious person who believed he had fulfilled the commandments of God by treating those like himself as his neighbours. The parable is a sharp reminder of how easily religious practice can turn into self-interest. The priest and the Levite were too concerned with their own safety, their concerns for ritual purity, and getting to Jerusalem to fulfil their religious duties to help another human being. It is the outsider, the Samaritan, who demonstrates that the dynamics of the community God calls into being are based upon the love that crosses boundaries, even at risk and cost to self.

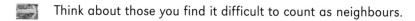 Think about those you find it difficult to count as neighbours.

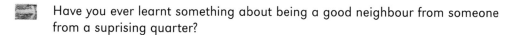 Have you ever learnt something about being a good neighbour from someone from a suprising quarter?

In a multicultural society being a good neighbour goes beyond the tolerance of people who are different from us. It requires the building of relationships and courage in the face of difference.

 Think of someone whose vision differs from yours.

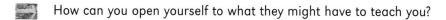 How can you open yourself to what they might have to teach you?

Gracious God,
do not surround me with people who agree with me before I speak;
I need true companions and not shadows.
Save me from needing always to be right,
I need room to try new thoughts and ways to be.
And when I meet someone with whom I disagree
give me courage to struggle shoulder to shoulder,
confident that in the encounter new gifts will be received.
Amen.

Day 6
Church as guest

These things I remember as
*   I pour out my soul:*
how I went with the throng,
and led them in procession
*   to the house of God,*
with glad shouts and songs
*   of thanksgiving,*
a multitude keeping festival.
Why are you so cast down,
*   O my soul,*
and why are you disquieted
*   within me?*
Hope in God; for I shall
*   again praise him,*
my help and my God.

Psalm 42.4–5

In the past this monastery at Samos was one of the most powerful in Spain. Today there are only a few monks left living and worshipping in its vast shell. All over Europe, churches and Christian institutions are finding themselves on the edges of society where once they were influential.

The legacy of this influence in nation states and in local communities is that many churches are used to owning property, to supporting social projects and to seeing themselves as the centre of activity.

In a changed and changing situation churches need to find new ways of understanding themselves and communicating the gospel. Without the status of secular position or the confidence of a large crowd, churches need to relearn how to meet with others on their territory and to speak a language which can be readily understood.

 What signs do you see that the position of the Church in society has changed?

 How do you feel about these changes?

Jesus spent much of his time as the guest of others: at Cana, in the house of Martha, Mary and Lazarus, in the home of Simon Peter's mother-in-law. Many of his parables are about banquets or are told in the context of dinner parties, and Jesus himself was rebuked for dining with prostitutes and sinners like Zaccheus. Even the Last Supper Jesus hosted in a borrowed room.

 What kind of spirituality is required of a Church that sees itself as guest, rather than host?

Gracious God,
as our civilization turns,
help us to let go of the old landmarks and find you in new places.
As familiar ways of being church crumble,
teach us again that we are living stones.
As new gifts and skills are called forth from your people,
help us to step out in faith and follow where the Spirit of Christ leads.
Amen.

5: Coming Home
– from Astorga to Santiago de Compostela

The contemporary 'banda' serenades pilgrims as they enter the holy city, echoing the 24 saints from Revelation depicted in the eleventh-century 'Portico de Gloria' as they welcome home each pilgrim soul.

From Astorga to Santiago de Compostela

'O Ultreia!' 'To the end!' is the ubiquitous encouragement to pilgrims. It is painted on road signs and shouted from the cabs of lorries, and whispered by gnarled elderly women who, tending their goats, have seen generations of pilgrims pass. When the pilgrim sets out, arriving in Santiago seems a distant prospect. When asked if you are going all the way to Santiago, the traditional response is 'God willing', acknowledging the trials and tribulations and even fatal accidents that may prevent a safe arrival. The pilgrim travels hopefully for so long, that when the end comes into view it is difficult to know how to feel. The pilgrim has learned how to walk. What will it mean to arrive?

These were some of the thoughts that crept into my mind as the kilometres started to tick down into the hundreds. From the 100 km point, there are markers every kilometre, and suddenly time is running through the fingers like sand. The mind begins to focus on ending, upon saying goodbye to friends; upon what it will feel like to stop walking; upon the prospect, once so distant, of going home. For those who came on this pilgrimage to make decisions, the moment of choosing is approaching; for those who came hoping to make a life-adjustment, the time to focus on reintegration into life at home begins; for those who came with their minds open to a new experience, this is the time to review what it meant and what will be of lasting value.

I remember sitting on the steps of the church of St Nicholas at Portomarin, five days' walk from Santiago. The church itself has an amazing story to tell. A thirteenth-century church of architectural importance, it was moved stone by stone from the bottom of the valley when it was flooded to make the reservoir that now borders the west of the town. The church was saved because the tympanum above the west door was sculpted by di Mateo, the master-sculptor whose 'Gate of Glory' dominates the cathedral of Santiago, with its 24 saints arced above the entrance, playing their harps and hurdy-gurdies.

Here, in Portomarin, five days short of Santiago, are the same saints with their harps and hurdy-gurdies in miniature, focusing the pilgrim's mind on the few days left before they must be ready to arrive. The scene is one of celebration, sending the mind towards the sound of the Galician pipes and drums that are still played by bands in the towns and villages of this Celtic people and which sound long into the night in the square at Santiago. The stones depict the celebration of heaven which is reflected in the earthly celebrations at arriving safely, at reunion with friends, at the achievement of walking so far and through so many trials and tribulations.

What were you hoping for when you began this book? What will you take away?

Yet di Mateo's saints – both in Santiago and at Portomarin – surround the figure of Christ in Judgement and remind the pilgrim that a pilgrimage is never only about the journey outwards, but that it is also about the journey inwards. The serious face of Christ poses the serious question 'Why did

107

you come?' Sitting on the steps of the church of St Nicholas, waiting for the floodlights to come on so that I could see the face of Christ just once before the ten o'clock hostel curfew, my serious answer was this: 'To learn to come home.'

For each pilgrim the answer to the question is different and yet for each serious pilgrim, here is a moment of judgement, a moment of truth, when fantasies are stripped away. From here, each pilgrim will have to return home – or choose not to. Each pilgrim will have to go back to face the empty house, or the job they have chosen to leave or the lifestyle they wanted to change. The road has allowed them space to be, to think, to grow. But who are they now? What have they learned? Now is the time to decide, 'Why did I come?'

Medieval pilgrims came in search of pardon or healing at the shrine of a saint, but what do contemporary pilgrims expect?

For medieval pilgrims the answers were focused upon the person of St James whose bones are (officially) buried in Santiago. They came to a holy place to seek pardon, to seek forgiveness, to seek healing. Some were sent by the civil or Church authorities as a punishment or a penance. They could not return to their own societies or receive Communion again until they had in their hands the proof of their pardon – a papal indulgence issued on their arrival at the shrine of St James. Some travelled to expiate their own sense of guilt, seeking forgiveness of their own accord, believing that an apostle, like St James, to whom Christ had once given authority to forgive sins, would be able to do so beyond the grave. Some, suffering from leprosy or other appalling diseases, came to find healing in the presence of holiness on earth in the form of a saint's bones.

The vestiges of these beliefs and practices are enshrined in the rituals of arriving in Santiago. The pilgrim queues to hug the statue of St James and to enter the crypt beneath to touch his coffin. The pilgrim office next door to the cathedral issues indulgences to any who produce their pilgrim passports and can prove they have walked at least 100 kilometres. The cathedral is lined with confessional boxes, ready to hear the confessions of those who come, not only on foot, but by the bus load, to worship in a holy place.

Are there any places you would name as 'holy'?

To the English, for whom cathedrals are austere places, which were stripped of the tombs of saints and the gold of shrines and the paraphernalia of pilgrimage at the Protestant Reformation, the scene feels medieval. Here is England before the Reformation. And yet here are contemporary men and women, hugging the effigy of a saint and weeping before a tomb. Here am I, an English Protestant brought up to be suspicious of idolatry, experiencing this as a profoundly holy place. What can this mean?

108

A holy place?

Christians have been ambivalent about the notion of holy places from earliest times. Hesitations about what it meant to designate one place as holier than any other were raised by the Church Fathers when shrines and relics became the focus of Christian devotion. Gregory of Nyssa, for example, stated that the grace of the Holy Spirit is not more abundant at Jerusalem than anywhere else, and warned people not to travel long distances searching for the grace of Christ that could be found at home. Yet the practice of pilgrimage was considered beneficial by him and others as long as it was understood to be an outward expression of longing for what St Paul describes as the Jerusalem from above (Galatians 4.26).

According to the Gospel of John, one of the fundamental beliefs of Christianity is that a holy place has been replaced by a holy person. Whereas the Holy of Holies in Jerusalem was, for the Jewish people of Jesus' day, the most holy place where heaven and earth might meet, according to John, Jesus reinterprets this place of holy meeting as his own body (John 2.18–22). Once ascended, therefore, the person of Jesus is accessible anywhere. Grace need not be mediated through any special person or place. The grace of God is available to anyone in any time or place through the person of Jesus Christ and the work of God's Spirit.

The theme is developed by the letter to the Hebrews which explains that the rites of the Temple and the Holy of Holies itself are mere copies or sketches of heavenly things, whereas Christ has actually entered into heaven on behalf of the human race, once and for all (Hebrews 9-10).

In the New Testament a holy place is made subordinate to the person of Jesus Christ. If places have a role it is as reminders or symbols of his grace. There can be no sense in which place provides access to holiness which is separate from the grace of Christ. If this is true of place then it is also true of people. A holy person is holy only by virtue of being in Christ – they have no holiness of their own which can heal the devotee, only access to the grace of Christ. So, for example, when Peter and John heal the lame man outside the Beautiful Gate (Acts 3), they do so in and the through the power of Christ. They act as conduits for a transforming holiness which they do not possess and is not their own. As Peter and John aligned themselves with the healing grace of God in Christ, so they were able to become the means through which that grace was communicated to another human being.

For the guardians of the tomb of St James writing in the twelfth century, this channelling of grace was possible, not just through the living, but through the dead. If Christ had once given the authority to St James to forgive sins when he breathed his Holy Spirit on his apostles after the resurrection (John 20.22–23), why would he take it away at his death? So, it was believed that 'whoever goes truly penitent to St James and asks for his help with all his heart will certainly have all his sins blotted out'.[10] The tangible proof that the sinner had come, penitent, all the way to Santiago, and asked for forgiveness was the plenary indulgence, wiping the sinner's slate clean.

109

There are a whole host of reasons why it is difficult for contemporary minds to enter into a world in which the relics of saints were sincerely believed to channel grace to those in search of healing and pardon. The sale of indulgences and the shameless profiteering associated with shrines mean that it is difficult, even for Catholic pilgrims today, to treat the indulgence they receive on arriving in Santiago as anything more than evidence that they completed the pilgrimage.

For Protestants there is the suspicion that neither the granting of indulgences nor the veneration of saints is biblical, and a nagging worry that the rites of arrival in Santiago are not only unnecessary but possibly idolatrous – putting St James in the place of Christ who is the only one

Have you ever experienced a tomb or grave as a gateway to heaven?

who can forgive sins. And then there is something counterintuitive for contemporary western people about expecting healing from a dead body. For us, corpses are associated with disease and not with healing.

Rationally it may be difficult for contemporary people to make sense of the cult of relics, and yet it was the conviction of the Christian world from the late Roman period through to the High Middle Ages that holy people, the places they had lived, and their physical remains were thresholds at which God's healing and grace might be encountered.

As I hugged the statue of St James and the tears ran down my cheeks, what did I make of all this? Did I expect St James to offer me forgiveness? As I received my indulgence, endorsed still by Pope John Paul II, even though he too was now dead, did I believe I was pardoned? Was the tomb of St James, for me, as for my medieval fellow pilgrims, a threshold at which God's healing and grace might be encountered?

For early Christians the saints retained a powerful presence at their tombs because Jesus' death and resurrection had brought the living and the dead into a new relationship.

My own insight into the potential importance of the tomb of a believer as a place of encounter began to develop at the tomb of Martin Luther King Jr when I visited Atlanta as a theological student. I remember escaping from the university library on one long, sunny afternoon, and travelling on the metro into the centre of town. After a few false starts, wandering around the rather intimidating district of the inner city in which he was minister, I found the Martin Luther King Junior Centre for Peace Studies.

The classrooms are built around a central pool. In the centre of the pool is Martin's tomb. I sat in the shade, leaning on a pillar, looking at his tomb, and I began to read *Trumpet of Conscience*. Slowly reading his essays in close proximity to his physical remains made it clear to me that this was not an academic exercise. Sitting here, where he had lived and was buried, I was acutely aware of this legend of a man as a real person who lived and died and made choices. Travelling to downtown Atlanta to be in the presence of his memory arose not just from a desire to understand him, but was the expression of a desire to be like him. My physical presence near his physical remains became a gateway through which I could glimpse a radical kind of discipleship which might risk even death.

For the early Christians the saints retained a powerful presence at their tombs, partly because of the Christian belief in the resurrection of the body. Jesus Christ, through his embodiment in human flesh and his bodily resurrection, had brought the living and the dead into a new relationship. The dead bodies of faithful disciples were not unclean as they had been to the Jews, but rather brought believers within touching distance of resurrection. The saints and martyrs who had died were in touch with the face of God yet, through their bones, were still located on earth, offering gateways through which heaven could be glimpsed. Indeed, from the early centuries through to the Middle Ages, a church could only be founded on the burial site of a genuine saint. Even today, it is part of the canon law of the Roman Catholic Church that every altar should contain the relics of a disciple of Christ, publicly acknowledged as such by the official process of canonization.

St James is such a saint. He was one of the 12 disciples. The son of Zebedee, he was the brother of John. Like the other disciples he knew Jesus intimately; with them he listened to Jesus' teaching and struggled to understand what Jesus was saying and who Jesus was. He witnessed the transfiguration of Jesus on the mountain top and thought he could follow Jesus until the end. With his brother, John, he asked to sit at the places of honour with Jesus in heaven, and had to learn that leadership is about service and not about glory. At the crucifixion he had to come to terms with his own betrayal and cowardice, retreating, with the other disciples, behind locked doors for fear of the Jews. And yet, transformed by his experience of the risen Christ and the outpouring of his Spirit, he risked his life and finally lost it for the sake of the gospel: according to Acts 12.2 he was executed by Herod in 63 AD.

Beyond these few facts, little is known of St James the Greater, although legends abound. The story of how St James comes to be the patron saint of Spain is told in storyboard form in the cathedral at Santiago: commissioned by Jesus himself, at the end of Matthew's Gospel, James sets out for Spain. In fact it is probably the result of a scribal error that James was ever thought to be in Spain at all, but the tradition holds that he was the first to evangelize the Iberian peninsula before returning to the Holy Land to be martyred. The story then goes that James' fellow disciples then despatched his body in a coracle which made its way, with the help of angels, along the Mediterranean Sea and into the Atlantic, eventually finding its way up the course of a river to be buried on the site where Santiago's cathedral is now situated.

Identification with St James is an important part of the story of the pilgrimage to Santiago. It was not a dimension of the Camino that I had anticipated. I was surprised, for example, to hear even quite apparently secular people report that they chose to talk to St James as they walked along. I was surprised, too, that the vast majority of those making this journey – whether they were Christian believers or not – wanted to identify themselves as pilgrims by wearing the traditional emblems. One possible interpretation of this behaviour is that it illustrates the postmodern playing with identity that was discussed in Chapter 1. Playing at being a pilgrim is simply another example of postmodern people without fixed identities trying on the pilgrim costume, like children playing in a dressing-up box. Yet identification with saints has been an important part of pilgrimage since its origins.

Identification with the saints has been an important dimension of Christian pilgrimage since its origins.

In the late classical period, for example, as the tradition of patron saints developed, identification with a saint was an important part of growing into a Christian identity. The poetry of Paulinus about St Felix of Nola speaks about the saint as the guardian of his identity, almost as if it were an unconscious layer of Paulinus' self, so closely had he identified with him. After Felix's death, far from the effect diminishing, Paulinus found time spent at Felix's grave helped him to feel connected with his own identity in Christ. Because Felix, in his death, was now intimately united with Christ, Paulinus found meditation at his tomb to be almost like being present at the gate of heaven.

Who have played important roles in the development of your Christian faith?

Much in the way that contemporary spirituality is fascinated by the idea of guardian angels who will protect the individual in this life and in the life to come, it might be easy to dismiss this late classical instinct for adopting a patron saint as being a way of trying to establish powerful friends in heaven in the same way that classical patrons were necessary powerful friends on earth. In addition, another concern about the role of saints, highlighted by the Protestant Reformers has been that asking the saints to intercede for us makes it appear that the reconciliation effected by Christ is not sufficient. It seems to devalue grace. However, for St Augustine, writing in the classical period, when patron saints and the choosing of baptismal names were important, there was another important dimension. He wrote, 'Men who had shown themselves, as martyrs, to be true servants of God, could bind their fellow men even closer to God than could the angels.'[11] Rather than our faith being weakened by association with the saints, he believed that making a bond with those who have lived the life of Christ authentically and persuasively in ways that make sense to us can inspire us to work out what it means to live the Christian gospel authentically in our own lives.

Making a bond with those who have lived the Christian life authentically can help us work out how to live out the gospel in our own lives.

This is what was happening for Paulinus in his devotion to St Felix; it was true for me in getting to know Martin Luther King Jr. Is this, then, what was going on for those pilgrims who were queuing to touch the tomb of St James? Had they recognized in him a fellow companion in faith who could help them to make sense of their own pilgrimage through life? Was I was hugging his statue and washing his shoulders with my tears because I had found through him a profound connection to Christ? Or was it that they, or I, expected something much more direct from this saint? Were we expecting from him a miracle of forgiveness or healing?

Miracles of healing?

There is no doubt that one of the dangers of identifying the tomb of a saint as a place where the veil is thin is that it can lead to the expectation of miracles on demand. Indeed, medieval pilgrimage sites were established on the basis of the miracles thought to have been performed by a saint. In the language of the twenty-first century, travelling to a shrine in the hope that a saint will perform a miracle sounds like a version of cosmic ordering – stating what one wants and believing in it will result in the desired effect – unfortunately for the Spanish football team, stopping off at Santiago to pray before playing in the European Cup finals in Portugal in 2004, the magic did not work and they went out in the group stage of the tournament.

Perhaps some of my fellow pilgrims were expecting miraculous interventions in their lives, orchestrated by St James; perhaps they experienced them; perhaps, the experience of forgiveness or healing at the tomb of a saint depends on whether we come ready to receive. I know, for myself, that my arrival in Santiago as a pilgrim, having walked for weeks towards the moment,

Do you pray for healing? What kind of answer do you hope for?

was a very different experience from visiting the tomb of St Peter in Rome. In Rome I was a tourist. I was interested and curious, but not deeply moved. In Santiago, I was a pilgrim, all my cells open, ready to listen, ready to be re-formed, ready to receive. The miracle of healing I experienced was that of reconciliation.

I arrived in the cathedral square amid hundreds of pilgrims and tourists, serenaded by buskers, photographed by those wanting a picture of a genuinely dirty, sweaty, well-laden pilgrim. There was plenty to look at and to delight in and yet my attention was focused only in one place. Until I had reached the tomb of St James, I had not arrived. I made my way to the great double staircase on the west front of the cathedral and began my ascent. The boots and the rucksack weighed me down up the steep steps and I thought heavily of all I carry and of all the miles I had come. And then I turned the corner of this magnificent hinged staircase and was faced with the statue of David playing his harp. Suddenly I was overwhelmed with a sense of all who help me carry what is mine – my friends, the saints, Christ himself. And in the turning on the stairs was the moment of repentance: the moment in which I knew myself willing, at last, to be defined, not by grief anymore, but by grace. Suddenly, though no less heavy, somehow the rucksack had become my own. No longer desperate to be rid of what I carried, I was prepared to receive who I am. I knew myself accepted, loved and forgiven. I looked up at the 24 saints from the book of Revelation, arced in stone above my head and rejoiced with them in the knowledge that I was ready to be welcomed home.

In one sense, this knowledge was nothing new. All the way from the Pyrenees I carried the knowledge that I am forgiven, loved and free. This is knowledge with which I have lived for, perhaps, 30 years. Since I was 11 I have believed that I am loved by God and forgiven all that keeps me from his presence and from right relationship with others. The journey for me since I first understood the Christian gospel has been one of deeper and deeper acceptance of this truth, that I might live more profoundly out of its life-giving power. My ability to push it away and live out of some less demanding freedom never ceases to amaze me. My ability to think that there are things about me too awful to bring to consciousness because to do so will separate me from the love of God is beyond telling. What I need, again and again, is space to come to terms more deeply with who I am, and the opportunity to receive more deeply the assurance that I am beloved.

The journey from the Pyrenees was a journey deeper into the truth of myself. It provided the space in which to become more fully aware of the dimensions of myself, my humanity, my limits, my drivenness, my fears. The journey provided a context in which to acknowledge my own lack of trust and lack of grace and need for love. The arrival in Santiago provided the opportunity for me to hear that what I had learned about myself still could not separate me from the love of God in Christ Jesus.

In that sense, St James provided the meeting place. His physical remains provided a place to walk to; offered the spacing of time and place in which to become more fully myself; his shrine offered me a place to stop and remember why I had come. I had come not just to know myself better, but to know more deeply that I am beloved of God. I had come to receive the indulgence, which now stands on my bookcase as a tangible reminder, like the cross emblazoned on my forehead at my baptism, that I am forgiven, loved and free.

The tomb of St James still provides a meeting place between pilgrims and the God who seeks to welcome them home.

The tomb of St James is holy for me, not in the same ways, perhaps, that it was holy for those medieval pilgrims whose feet before mine had worn down the scallop shell steps to St James' tomb; and not in the same ways that it is for some of my fellow pilgrims. And yet judging by the depth of the healing I experienced, it would not surprise me to meet those for whom becoming whole had involved not just spiritual wholeness but physical healing too.

The gospel stories bear witness to the connection between the spiritual healing of forgiveness and physical healing. Jesus heals the sick and forgives sins; the two are often interwoven and yet the connection is not straightforward – one does not always entail the other. There can be no excuse for explaining the lack of physical healing in any individual as being due to sin. Jesus, in the case of the man born blind, makes it clear that physical illness or disability is not a punishment for sin (John 9.3). Yet miracles of physical healing do take place in his ministry as men and women open themselves to transformation by grace. This is a far cry from miracles on demand, and a far cry from a belief in a God who does magic tricks. Rather, it evidences what Christians have experienced through the centuries, that those who seek to be drawn into the circle of God's redeeming power, and in so doing are prepared to be transformed, find healing and grace coursing through them in unexpected ways.

I did not come to Santiago expecting a miracle of healing whereby God suspends the laws of nature and through the mortal remains of a saint reaches out to heal the body, but neither did I come with the modernist belief that God is distant and divorced from encounter in real time and place. I came convinced, and became more and more convinced along the way, that the God who crackles beneath the surface of the whole creation, waiting for us to be ready to meet with him, knows our struggle to come home and provides for us means of grace by which we might draw near to him.

A means of grace

In this way the shrine at Santiago is a means of grace. It is a place in which generations of people have encountered God before; a place in which others are encountering God; a place in which the cells of our being might be open to healing and forgiveness. To claim that there is spiritual value in the pilgrimage to the shrine of a saint is not to claim that God is more present there than at home. Rather because human beings are creatures in time and space, it is to say that we need structured help to be attentive to the presence of the God who is everywhere and at all times longing to meet us and welcome us home.

John Wesley understood this and expressed it in his sermon 'The Means of Grace'. He commended to his hearers the outward signs, words or actions which God has appointed for conveying grace, such as prayer, reading the Bible and receiving the Lord's Supper. He was not arguing that any of these means have power in themselves, any more than do the bones of a saint, but he urged his hearers to attend to God through them. In other parts of the Church these means are called *sacramenta* or ordinances: those outward words and actions through which the grace of God can be appropriated.

Thus pilgrimage, like Holy Communion, provides an opportunity for encountering Christ. As the story of the Last Supper is told and as the bread and wine are consecrated and as the communicant walks down the aisle to the rail, their attention is funnelled towards the God who draws near to us; an occasion is made which God honours; the Christian is re-membered as part of the body of Christ across the world and through the ages. In the same way a shrine can draw people into the presence of God and into the body of believers.

What outward signs help sustain you in your faith and make occasions for encounter with God?

115

This truth is profoundly enacted in the last of the rituals in which the pilgrim is invited to engage on arrival at the cathedral of Santiago: the placing of their hands in the genealogy of Christ. The tree of Jesse is the part of the 'Gate of Glory' – that glorious stonework screen of the Last Judgement sculpted by di Mateo – a plasterwork copy of which can be seen in the Victoria and Albert Museum in London. The screen is formed of several arches, supporting the apostles; above the arches sits Christ in Glory, surrounded by the traditional symbols of the four evangelists: the angel of St Matthew, the lion of St Mark, the calf of St Luke and the eagle of St John. Around him, like a rainbow, sit the 24 elders from Revelation, playing their harps and lutes and hurdy-gurdies. Below Christ in judgement the supporting pillar is carved as a tree of Jesse.

From Adam to Jesus, from floor to rafter, the story of God is woven into the story of humanity. Here, generation upon generation of God's dealings with saints and sinners are recorded, taken from the genealogies in the Gospels of Luke and Matthew: here is Jacob, the cheat, and Tamar, who was raped, and David, the adulterer, and Rahab, the prostitute, and countless other complex, compromised, faithful and faithless people – none of whom are written out of the story – but all of whom are redeemed in Christ who sits at the top of the pillar, willing to welcome any who would be woven into his story of salvation.

As I reached the head of the queue, I placed my hand on the pillar as those before me have done through the years, and my hand disappeared into the stone – the hole worn smooth and deep by the hands of centuries – and I wept to be welcome in this family tree of Christ, alongside all those who have come before, and even those yet to come. I wept to realize that here am I in the company of those who are fully human as I am. Here, grafted into the family tree of Christ, in which there is no need to pretend, it is safe to be known and to be loved.

Amazing grace

It is not necessary to walk in order to know God as our home, but the discipline of pilgrimage is a reminder for any who would walk in spirit that the only distance to be crossed into God's loving presence is the journey into our own reality.[12] Only here is God able to meet us as prodigal sons and daughters, because only as the people we really are can we be welcomed home.

Pilgrimage is a reminder that the only distance to be crossed into God's loving presence is the journey into our own reality.

Perhaps the necessity to go on pilgrimage is because so often this amazing grace is turned by churches into a demand for perfection or respectability. Somewhere in the backs of our minds we turn the Christian life into a discipline which is an end in itself and life becomes an exhausting round of justifying our place at the table of God's banquet. It is a doomed project. No one can earn God's grace; and no one becomes Christlike through trying harder. We begin to feel like the elder son of the prodigal father: we become resentful of those who have not tried as hard as we have; who have not conformed as we have; who have not sacrificed as much as we have. Anger and resentment boil up inside us. We start to try to cover our tracks. The Christian life becomes about covering up who we really are and how we really feel, and is not about the relief of being known and loved. We forget that the Christian life stems from the joy of the knowledge that God loves us and is an invitation further into that joy.

So much of this book has been about the narrowness of the way. So much of it has been about the way of the cross. So much of it has been about the pain of self-discovery that pilgrimage could be interpreted as a form of self-harm, or worse, as a way of allowing God to punish us for our sins: a discipline which is death-dealing and not life-giving. Although the image of the suffering Christ is at the heart of the Christian gospel, however, suffering is never for its own sake and God takes no pleasure in it. Christ endures the cross and invites us to pick up our own only for the sake of the redemption of the whole creation.

Christians need ocasions for remembering and communicating the joy of life in Christ.

For this reason, it is important in living the Christian life that we allow ourselves, not only to be drawn into the death of Christ and the sacrificial way of the cross, but that we allow ourselves also to be drawn into the joy of Christ's risen life. When I first visited Santiago, I arrived in Holy Week. The cathedral square was full of penitents in guild costumes, marching barefoot through the snow between floats picturing scenes from Christ's Passion. These are scenes enacted every year throughout Spain and they are powerful occasions for allowing Christ's suffering to resonate with our own. The second year in which I witnessed such processions was the year of the Madrid bombings. Watching the hundreds of Spanish people who had turned out to witness the processions weeping at the sight of Mary standing at the foot of the cross brought home to me the power of such identification. But what, I wondered, would open up for these people the joy of resurrection?

This is an important question for Christians of all traditions to address. It may be necessary for us to communicate to contemporary people that there is value in the discipline of a narrow way, but we need also to communicate the depth of joy that such a narrow way facilitates. We need to take care that we do not spend more time in our sermons and outreach programmes talking about sin and suffering and sacrifice than we do about forgiveness and healing and gift. Although questions of judgement and justice cannot be glossed over, they need to be rooted in a conviction that God is for us; any encouragement to us to endure the pain of self-discovery and the stripping away of false securities must be motivated by the love expressed in the prayer attributed to St Paul, 'that [we] may have the power to comprehend, with all the saints, what is the breadth and length and height and depth, and to know the love of Christ that surpasses knowledge, so that [we] may be filled with all the fullness of God' (Ephesians 3.18–19).

The experience of arriving in Santiago was, for me, an occasion for realizing that God rejoices at our homecomings. It was reflected in the faces of the saints in stone, gazing at each other, each with a hand on part of the hurdy-gurdy, smiling attentively at each other and mirroring the attentiveness depicted by Rublev's icon of the Trinity as being at the heart of God's very self. It was played out in the Mass, when at noon each day the names of those who have travelled to this place as pilgrims are read out, like the names written in the book of the Lamb. It was crystallized as I met up with David and Christina, and Dorothea and Breton and Pam and Leona, and so many of my fellow pilgrims, the complexity of whose stories I was only beginning to know.

What God seeks for us is holiness. The road to holiness is a costly path for it requires that we surrender all that keeps us from the God who is holy and just and good. Yet God's only wish for us is the wholeness for which we, in our better moments, also long. In her book, *Miss Garnet's Angel*, Salley Vickers paints the picture of a woman who in retirement exiles herself to Venice. The book tells the story of what she learns about herself in a foreign city. One day she sits in St Mark's and wonders what it is that makes a place holy. 'Is it,' she wonders, 'a place in which to become whole again?'

Wholeness is not something we, as individuals, can possess. Wholeness does not mean the process of sticking back together all the parts of us that have become fragmented, as if they had never been estranged. Rather, wholeness is about realizing the healing that comes from knowing ourselves part of a much bigger whole.

Wholeness is about realizing that healing comes from knowing ourselves part of a much bigger whole.

The realization began as I placed my feet in the snowprints left by pilgrims before me, showing the way over the Pyrenees. It was one of many signs that the pilgrimage continues, and that individuals become part of it for a time, adding their story to its thousand-year narrative, snaking across the landscape, finding their place, belonging. It is not just that the pilgrimage has become part of me, but that I have become part of the pilgrimage.

How would you describe what it is to be holy or to be whole? How are they related?

The realization developed as I knelt in the red mud of the plains of Léon, listening to the frogs chirruping in the stream; realizing that I too am made from the dust of the earth; that we together are nature, created, cared for and being redeemed by the God who weaves all things together for good for those who love him.

The realization crystallized as I placed my hand in the genealogy of Christ, feeling the stone, smoothed by millions of hands, knowing myself part of the family tree of Christ that stretches across continents and generations; realizing that my life is held together, not by me, in all my desperate attempts to edit and re-edit my story, but by the God who knows and loves the whole of creation.

Not every pilgrim is ready, when they arrive in Santiago, to be welcomed into the joy of Christ's risen life. Not every time that a pilgrim makes the journey will they experience the same healing and peace. Even if the experience is profound, the journey of life and faith and doubt continues and further means of grace will be needed. For although God may be powerfully encountered at a shrine, and on the journey towards one, God is not trapped in stone, nor confined to a tomb. God, in Christ, is ever-present to us, coming out to meet us, longing for us to realize that our hearts are restless until they find their rest in him.

Day 1

The mountain of joy

All of these died in faith without having received the promises, but from a distance they saw and greeted them. They confessed that they were strangers and foreigners on the earth, for people who speak in this way make it clear that they are seeking a homeland.

Hebrews 11.13–15

The Mount of Joy is so named because this is the first point from which the pilgrim can see the distant cathedral spires. To see the long-longed for destination is a moving moment which promises welcome and rest and a sense that we belong. Longing is a feature of pilgrimage. The word itself suggests distance – a long way to be travelled – and belonging – a sense that part of us is already in the far country. St Augustine valued pilgrimage as a physical way of refining our longing for God and honing our sense that we belong in God's presence.

   Try to make an uncensored list of the things you long for.

Some of the things we long for are basic human needs, without which our hearts will always be restless – acceptance; forgiveness; release from pain; permission to be ourselves; space to grow and become – these are the things that God is longing to give us. Yet it is easy to focus these longings on more immediate objects: we yearn for more power so that we can escape the pain of a humiliation; we long for relationships as ways of finding acceptance and love, yet we do so by trying to be the people others want us to be; we long for bigger houses and faster cars as a way of managing the deeper longings that we are afraid to face.

Yearning for these things can give them such a power over us that they begin to possess us. We begin to mark our lives by their progress towards these destinations, only to find that each time we arrive, our longing is not satisfied.

   Bring what you long for to God.

   Ask God to help you discern what is worth longing for.

Lord, our hearts are restless until they find their rest in you.
In all that we long for, grant us discernment
that we may toil for bread that will satisfy
and living water that will last. Amen.

121

Day 2
Laying aside every weight

Therefore, since we are surrounded by so great a cloud of witnesses, let us also lay aside every weight and the sin that clings so closely, and let us run with perseverance the race that is set before us, looking to Jesus, the pioneer and perfecter of our faith, who for the sake of the joy that was set before him endured the cross, disregarding its shame, and has taken his seat at the right hand of the throne of God.

Hebrews 12.1–2

As the pilgrim climbs the final steps of the journey, this is the moment of truth. At the top of the steps sits Christ in judgement. His serious face asks of the pilgrim the serious question, 'Why did you come?' The subject of judgement can make us uncomfortable. If this is because there are things in our lives that we know we are being called to change, then we must change them. The writer to the Hebrews asks us to leave behind what we do not need to carry in order to enter into the joy of the kingdom. Some of the things that we carry are things we cannot change – these are wounds we must learn to live with and even to love – but some of what we carry is our own responsibility and need not be borne any longer. We need to remember that God's judgement is for us. Christ came into the world not to condemn us, but to save us from the worst of ourselves that we may know his risen life.

 Bring to mind the unchangeable facts of your life that you sometimes wish could be otherwise.

 What in yourself do you still need to accept and love as God loves?

Some of what we carry belongs to us and needs to be embraced. Yet there are other burdens that we carry unnecessarily.

 Bring to God those feelings and attitudes that weigh you down and feel as if they will never change.

 Pray for the strength to lay down those feelings and attitudes that keep you from experiencing new life.

Jesus our Judge,
all things have been put into your hands.
At times of judgement remind us that you have travelled the road we travel
and know us in our need.
Teach us to accept ourselves as you accept us.
Show us the weight that clings to us and that needs to be discarded.
Grow in us a love for life in all its fullness,
that we may know the joy of resurrection, even now.
Amen.

Day 3
Joy in heaven

After this I looked, and there in heaven a door stood open! At once I was in the spirit, and there in heaven stood a throne, with one seated on the throne! And the one seated there looks like jasper and cornelian and around the throne is a rainbow that looks like an emerald. Around the throne are twenty-four thrones, and seated on the thrones are twenty-four elders, dressed in white robes, with golden crowns on their heads; they cast their crowns before the throne, singing, 'You are worthy, our Lord and God, to receive glory and honour and power.'
Revelation 4.1a, 2–4, 10b–11

124

The gateway to the cathedral at Santiago is a thirteenth-century carving of this scene from the book of Revelation. It is a scene of pure joy. Each elder plays an instrument, and each face reflects the joy on the faces of the pilgrims beneath, as they look up in awe and amazement at this ancient depiction of the party that is heaven.

Santiago is full of parties. Pilgrims separated on the road greet and embrace one another and share one another's delight at having arrived. Buskers play in the streets, welcoming tourists and pilgrims alike. Worship each lunchtime celebrates the safe arrival of another batch of pilgrims with song and Holy Communion, that foretaste of the heavenly banquet. The vision of heaven in the 'Portico de Gloria' is enacted below: a banquet, a celebration, a community remade.

Sometimes in the Church, even our depictions of heaven can be drab and over-serious. The worship of heaven is envisaged as a tedious and never-ending duty. The gate of heaven is a narrow one at which, if we are lucky, we shall be admitted by the skin of our teeth. The joy of God at the lost being found and the broken made whole is overlooked as we focus on the need for repentance. But here in Santiago, among the pilgrims of today and in the stones of a thousand years, heaven is a place for deep rejoicing.

How do you picture heaven?

How appealing is that picture?

In the book of Revelation worship characterizes the life of heaven. It is not dull or draining for it involves being fully ourselves and giving fully of ourselves. This is life in all its fullness.

Call to mind moments when you have felt fully yourself or have been able to give yourself fully to a person or task.

Allow these moments to be for you glimpses of heaven as you pray Charles Wesley's prayer:

Finish then thy new creation, pure and spotless let us be;
Let us see thy great salvation, perfectly restored in thee:
Changed from glory into glory, till in heaven we take our place,
Till we cast our crowns before thee, lost in wonder, love and praise![13]

Day 4

You have died and your life is hidden with Christ

Now to him who by the power at work within us is able to accomplish abundantly far more than all we can ask or imagine, to him be glory in the church and in Christ Jesus to all generations, for ever and ever. Amen.

Ephesians 3.20–21

One of the rituals of arrival in Santiago is to place your hand where generations of pilgrims have placed theirs, into the genealogy which rises from Adam to Christ. Becoming Christian is about being grafted into the adoptive family of Jesus Christ. Yet the family of Christ is not set apart from the families from which we come. In Christ, God has identified with the whole human family in all its mess and shame. The family tree of Jesus includes those who have sinned and those who have been sinned against. Whoever we are and whatever secrets we carry or are buried in our family histories there is room for us in the family tree of Christ.

 Think back over your own family history or your own life's history.

 Call to mind both the stories that are proudly told and the stories that are glossed over.

To belong to Christ does not require pretending that we are not part of the human network of sin and hurt in which we often cannot tell where the trail of damage began. To belong to Christ is to be brought into a new relationship with our families and our histories as one who bears with others and allows oneself to receive forgiveness. In the case of those we have hurt and those who have hurt us deeply, sometimes we cannot be in touch, yet in Christ we are called to yearn for the healing even of those with whom we cannot yet bear.

 Pray for those with whom your life has been bound up, especially any from whom you are estranged. Pray for the will to seek their good.

Gracious God,
when we are ashamed of ourselves and want to hide from the hurt we have caused to others,
help us to open our hearts to the depths of your healing grace.
When we want to separate ourselves from those who have hurt us, or from those of whom we are ashamed, remind us that our healing is bound with theirs.
When we are bound to others only by agony
bind us with your grace,
that together in Christ we may be whole.
Amen.

Day 5
Watch over one another in love

My brothers and sisters, if anyone among you wanders from the truth and is brought back by another, you should know that whoever brings back a sinner from wandering will save the sinner's soul from death and will cover a multitude of sins.

James 5.19-20

Since the ninth century pilgrims have come to the shrine of St James looking for healing and forgiveness. The letter of James exhorts those who know the love of Christ to watch over their brothers and sisters: to anoint them with oil when they are sick, to pray for them, and to lift them up so that their sins will be forgiven, especially those who have wandered from the path. For some pilgrims, it is St James who has watched over them, anointed them in their sickness, prayed for them and lifted them up to God so that their sins will be forgiven. For others it is the living to whom they will be eternally grateful for bringing them back home.

The Christian life is not a solitary life. Many of us were introduced to the life of faith by other Christians who not only told us about Jesus Christ but embodied for us what an authentic Christian life might look like in our own day and age. Although we may rarely be aware of it, an unbroken chain of witness connects us with the first apostles, like St James, who first lived and spread the good news. Some of these fellow pilgrims may have been our parents or peers. Others we may have encountered through their writings or in the stories of the Bible, or in our prayers.

 Look back over your life. Recall the faces and names of those who have introduced you to Christ and who have helped you keep the faith.

It is one thing to see others as saints who have helped us to live the Christian life. It is a more daunting thing to realize that we may be the saints whom God is calling to embody the Christian way for others.

 Who do you know who has left the Church or is struggling with it?

 How might you keep in touch with them and continue to lift them before God?

We are pilgrims on a journey
and companions on the road,
we must learn to help each other
walk the mile and bear the load.[14]

129

Day 6
The gate of heaven

Then Jacob awoke from his sleep and said, 'Surely the Lord is in this place and I did not know it!' And he was afraid and said, 'How awesome is this place! This is none other than the house of God, and this is the gate of heaven.' So Jacob rose early in the morning, and he took the stone that he had put under his head and set it up for a pillar and poured oil on the top of it. He called that place Bethel; but the name of the city was Luz at the first.

Genesis 28.16–19

Whatever its origins and whatever its original name, like the Bethel of the Hebrew scriptures Santiago has grown as a place of pilgrimage because here people have encountered God. Each day of the year hundreds of people flock here to participate in Holy Communion, to make their confession, or to pray at the tomb of St James.

To many thousands of people, Santiago is a sacred place; a place where the veil between heaven and earth is thin; a place in which they have experienced the welcome of God; a place to which they will return time and again in person, or in imagination, in order to be in touch again with the blessing that there they received.

Many Christians speak about special places in their experience – places of encounter with God. Some keep photographs or other souvenirs of such places as a reminder to make the pilgrimage within themselves to that moment of encounter regularly. Making a physical journey to the place on an annual basis is another way of intentionally turning our attention towards the God who seeks encounter with us in all times and places.

 Think of moments in which you have glimpsed the welcome of God.

 What places of encounter have become special for you?

Although these places may hold important memories and have the power to act as meeting places with God because they connect us with our longing for him, a holy place is not a place where we can remain, but only a place we can visit. Pilgrims must come home to their ordinary lives, just as Jacob had to return from Bethel to his father's house. Yet if the experience of God has been authentic, we shall find that this God lives not only in the holy places we have visited, but among the complexities of our daily lives. And the sense that we have gained on the mountain top of what it is to be made whole and holy in God will burn in us as a touchstone of faith and hope and love for generations to come.

 How do you remember and mark these moments and places so that they continue to strengthen you for the ongoing journey?

Gracious God,
for all that has strengthened us on our journey this far,
we offer our thanks.
In all that lies ahead,
we entrust ourselves to you.
Amen.

131

Notes

Chapter 1

1. Zygmunt Bauman, *Postmodern Ethics*, Oxford: Blackwell, 1993, p. 240.
2. John Bell and Graham Maule, 'Will You Come and Follow Me?' © WGRG Iona Community.
3. *Methodist Worship Book*, Peterborough: Methodist Publishing House, 1999, pp. 288–89.

Chapter 2

4. James Nelson, *The Intimate Connection: Male Sexuality, Masculine Spirituality*, London: SPCK, 1992, p. 116.
5. George William Conder, 'All things praise thee, Lord most high'.
6. Dora Greenwell, 'And art thou come with us to dwell?'

Chapter 3

7. Eugenio Garibay Baños, written on the wall of a factory outside Najera.
8. Barbara Fairburn, unpublished poem.
9. Julie Hopkins, *Towards a Feminist Christology: Jesus of Nazareth, European Women and the Christological Crisis*, Kampen, Kok Pharos, 1994, p. 111.

Chapter 5

10. Sermon, 'Veneranda Dies' from the *Codex Calixtinus*.
11. Augustine of Hippo, *City of God*, X.16.
12. Rowan Williams, *Ponder these Things: Praying with Icons of the Virgin*, Norwich: Canterbury Press 2002, p. 30. He says, 'It is not that I have a long journey to make in order to get to God, but that I have a long journey to my own reality ... and pilgrimage is always travelling to where I am.'
13. Charles Wesley, 'Love divine, all loves excelling'
14. Richard Gilliard 'Brother, sister, let me serve you' © Scripture in Song, Kingsways Thank You Music.

Notes for Group Leaders

The pilgrimage of the Christian life is not a solitary journey, but one which needs companions. Although it is envisaged that those reading this book will undertake their own devotional journey as they read the chapters and work through the meditations, the notes in this section suggest ways of reading the book with a group – either within an existing Bible study or house group – or in a group which covenants to read the book together and meet weekly in order to discuss it and share something of their own pilgrimage of faith with each other.

Setting up a group

In order to work successfully with this material, it is important to discuss with the group their aims in using it. Clear expectations need to be established about the practicalities of the group's life (such as venue and for how long each session will last), as well as the ethos of the group. For example, if the meeting aims to be one where personal insights, questions and difficulties can be shared, the group needs to think about the kind of listening and confidentiality they need in order to make it safe enough for people to share in any depth.

Running a group

A group will work best with numbers of between 6 and 12. The larger the group, the more important it will be to allow people to discuss things in pairs or threes. Remember that this takes more time than a whole group discussion, but it does allow quieter members of the group to take a full part. It is not always necessary for small groups to feedback to the larger group. Each time you divide the group into smaller units, make the following things clear:
- The task the group has to do (write this on a flip chart that all can see or on a piece of paper that the group can have for reference).
- The time they have to do it in (you can write the finishing time on the flip chart too).
- Whether or not they will need to feedback to the wider group.

The structure of the sessions

The course is designed as 6 sessions of 1 hour and 45 minutes. (Although for each week there are two possible discussion topics, making a longer series possible if desired.) The structure of each session should follow a similar pattern. Detailed suggestions for each week are made below. Different people may like to take responsibility for food or worship. A group of two or three might like to plan the whole course and take turns in leading. However, do remember that continuity of leadership and style is an important factor in establishing a safe enough group for significant sharing and learning. It is not a good idea for anyone to lead – or become part of a group – who has not been part of establishing the covenant, as they will come with different expectations. It is a good idea to give yourself guideline times and keep checking your watch. You do not have to stick rigidly to these, but if the group is overrunning, you need to decide what to cut out so that people can get away at the agreed time. Groups that overrun tend to lose members.

Suggested skeleton structure

- Meal and informal conversation (45 minutes, optional).
- Opening worship (5 minutes).
- Review of the journey this week (20 minutes).
- Structured discussion. The suggestions for group work are designed to be used flexibly – it is not necessary for the group to discuss all the questions, or to complete both topics each time – use the time you have to suit the needs of the group (45 minutes will be enough to cover all the suggestions in either Structured discussion A or B).
- Pause for reflection (10–15 minutes).
- Group review. (5–10 minutes) Revisit the learning covenant and the record of people's hopes and expectations. Ask the group if there are any changes they want to make to the way the group is functioning. This is also an opportunity for you to comment on anything you feel has not been in the spirit of the covenant. Help people to work to what they have agreed, or to amend the agreement in a mutually acceptable way. Make any practical arrangements for next time.
- Closing prayers (5–10 minutes).

Preparing each session

Each week the leader needs to:
- Read the relevant chapter of the book and pray through at least some of the meditations.
- Look at the suggestions for group work listed under the relevant chapter heading below and decide which will work best for the group. In larger groups, if there is more than one group leader, the group could split in two, giving people a choice of material to work with.
- Ensure that all the relevant materials are available to complete the activities chosen (see notes below).
- Plan the set up of the room to facilitate the activities for the week.
- Plan the structure and timing of the session including any meal, worship and discussion time. Sometimes it is helpful for the whole group to have an idea of the structure of the session written out for them, with key questions and any additional worship material they need.

In addition:
- It is necessary for the group leader to be reading the group work material at least one week ahead of the schedule in order to be able to invite members to bring anything particular with them the following week: e.g. for Session 4 the group is asked to bring images of Jesus with them.
- It is a good practice for the leader to review how the group is going after each session and note anything they want to do differently next time.

Further suggestions to consider

It may be that your group is interested in further activities beyond weekly meetings. These are best discussed and dates agreed at the beginning of the course. Going on a physical journey together might be a good activity to help the group get to know each other better as well as entering more deeply into the imagery of pilgrimage.

- In medieval times, for those who could not go on a long pilgrimage, mini-pilgrimages were constructed around a monastic cloister or by creating a labyrinth on the floor of a cathedral. Organize a visit to a cathedral or church which has a labyrinth you can walk (the medieval ones are mostly in France, e.g. Chartres, Reims and St-Omer; English ones are mostly Victorian, e.g. at Ely Cathedral and in Itchen Stoke parish church. See www.labyrinthos.net/churchlabuk.htm for details). Make the journey part of the experience, marking the beginning and helping people prepare for the experience along the way with prayers and activities.

- Alternatively try constructing a mini-pilgrimage or labyrinth in a church or outside in a public space. (See Robert Ferré, *Praying the Chartres Labyrinth: a pilgrim's guidebook* or Helen Raphael Sands, *Walking the Healing Labyrinth*.) At each station provide a picture for people to look at, a Bible reading, a prayer or hymn with which to meditate, and an activity for people to engage in. Prepare a leaflet with clear instructions so that anyone can join in and move at their own pace.

- Many congregations will be familiar with 'The Stations of the Cross': a series of meditations on Jesus' walk to Golgotha, often marked on Good Friday by processing around a church and making prayers at each station. In the Easter season try constructing a service of 'Stations of the Resurrection'.

137

Planning Sessions 1-6

Read through all the following notes before you begin to make any plans. As you read, think about the people who are coming or might come to your group and make mental notes of things that will work and things that will need to be adapted to their needs.

Session 1: Introductory meeting

This is a session to help orient people to the course and to get to know each other. Only the leader needs to be familiar with the book before this session.

A meal may be shared (45 minutes) – preferably this should be in a home or other welcoming space, around a table – during which people get to know one another informally. Hospitality is an important dimension of pilgrimage. Traditionally pilgrims stayed in hostels where food, shelter, a fire and basic medical treatment were available. Think about how to make your guests welcome. In subsequent weeks, other group members may like to bring food to share with the group. This is something to discuss later when the group forms its covenant. A grace may be used such as that suggested here:

Gracious God,
all are welcome at the feast of your kingdom.
As you welcome us, help us to welcome one another
as fellow pilgrims and companions on the way.
In the name of Jesus Christ, the pioneer and perfecter of our faith.
Amen.

Setting up the room (allow 5–10 minutes to change the room or move rooms and for people to settle).

When the meal is finished, the group needs to clear the table, or move to another room which is arranged for group work. You will need:
- comfortable chairs arranged in a circle;
- Bibles in a modern translation;
- enough copies of the book for the group to have one each;
- a cloth, candle, ribbon and some shells for the focus point;
- flip chart and marker pens.

Place a tall candle in the centre of a cloth arranged on the floor in the centre of the group. Use a ribbon or rope to trace a path that winds around the candle and out towards the edge of the cloth. Provide a basket or plate of shells – a few more than there are participants – so that everyone can choose their own. (The traditional symbol of a pilgrim on the road to Santiago is a scallop shell. These are often available cheaply from fishmongers. Alternatively you could use shells from a local beach.)

Opening worship (10 minutes)

Draw the group together into worship using a quiet worship song or chant or some recorded music, e.g. 'Be still and know that I am God' (Anon); 'Be still, for the presence of the Lord, the holy one is here' by David J. Evans. Light the central candle.

Introduce the psalm: The destination of any Christian pilgrimage is deeper life with God. This is often symbolized as a holy city. When Jesus of Nazareth went on pilgrimage, the holy city was Jerusalem or Zion. One of the songs he would have sung on the way is Psalm 84. To long for Zion is to long for deeper communion with God.

Read Psalm 84 in unison together:

How lovely is your dwelling-place,
O LORD of hosts!
My soul longs, indeed it faints
for the courts of the LORD.

Even the sparrow finds a home,
and the swallow a nest for herself,
where she may lay her young,
at your altars, O LORD of hosts,
my King and my God.

Happy are those who live in your house,
ever singing your praise.

Happy are those whose strength is in you,
in whose heart are the highways to Zion.
As they go through the valley of Baca
they make it a place of springs;
the early rain also covers it with pools.
They go from strength to strength;
the God of gods will be seen in Zion.

O LORD God of hosts, hear my prayer;
give ear, O God of Jacob!
Behold our shield, O God;
look on the face of your anointed.
For a day in your courts is better
than a thousand elsewhere.
I would rather be a doorkeeper in
the house of my God
than live in the tents of wickedness.
For the LORD God is a sun and shield;
he bestows favour and honour.
No good thing does the LORD withhold
from those who walk uprightly.
O LORD of hosts,
happy is everyone who trusts in you.

Prayer:
As the deer pants for streams of living water,
so we long for you, O God.
As we have travelled through life,
we have glimpsed your face,
and the memory of those times is sweet.
As we gather now, to begin a journey together,
draw us to yourself.
Be the way on which we place our feet;
the truth we encounter in one another,
and the destination we seek,
for our hearts are restless
until they find their rest in you.
Amen.

Review of the journey: Where are we starting from? (10–15 minutes)

Books are distributed (if they have not been previously) and the leader makes a short statement of purpose:

> *Suggested aim: to meet together weekly to share our ongoing journey of faith.*

Invite participants to choose a shell. Explain that the shell is a symbol of their pilgrimage – as it is for pilgrims on the road to Santiago – and will be used throughout the course. As each person chooses a shell, they should introduce themselves to the group (if necessary), and share what they hope to receive from the group – a record of key words may be made on a flip chart.

Structured discussion (30–45 minutes depending on the size of the group)

Read Colossians 3.12–17:

> *As God's chosen ones, holy and beloved, clothe yourselves with compassion, kindness, humility, meekness, and patience. Bear with one another and, if anyone has a complaint against another, forgive each other; just as the Lord has forgiven you, so you also must forgive. Above all, clothe yourselves with love, which binds everything together in perfect harmony. And let the peace of Christ rule in your hearts, to which indeed you were called in the one body. And be thankful. Let the word of Christ dwell in you richly; teach and admonish one another in all wisdom; and with gratitude in your hearts sing psalms, hymns and spiritual songs to God. And whatever you do, in word or deed, do everything in the name of the Lord Jesus, giving thanks to God the Father through him.*

Give the group some guidance on reading the passage: In deciding to make a pilgrimage it is necessary to choose what to wear and what to pack. This is both literally and metaphorically true. It is not only the journey outwards that makes a pilgrimage, but the journey inwards. To travel as a pilgrim, therefore, entails clothing ourselves with a frame of mind in which we are open to God and open to others.

Invite the group to discuss in pairs what kinds of attitudes they need to clothe themselves with in order to undertake this pilgrimage.

Now, with the whole group, draw up an agreed covenant on a flip chart so that everyone can see what they are committing themselves to. Remind the group that whatever they hope to receive, they must also be willing to offer. It will be useful to have a record of this agreement of which everyone can have a copy. The group leader may need to remind participants of their agreement in the weeks to come.

Suggested themes that a covenant should include:

- Commitment to attend all the sessions (clarify dates, times, venues including any 'further activities' – see below).
- Commitment to pray for each other during the week as fellow companions on the way.
- Commitment to read the relevant chapter of the book in advance and use at least some of the meditations in personal devotion.
- Commitment to keep a prayer/reflective journal, noting down important questions and insights.
- Commitment to bring something of one's own faith journey to the group.
- Commitment to listen carefully to each other's experience.
- Willingness to learn from others.
- Appropriate confidentiality (personal information shared in the group should be confidential to the group and not repeated outside it).

Closing worship (15 minutes)

Read Ephesians 4.1–16.

Leader: *We are here to help one another towards deeper maturity in Christ. We have drawn up an agreement about how we will seek to build one another up. We commit ourselves to that agreement now, as we place our shells at the start of our pilgrimage together.*

Reflective music may be played.

When everyone is ready, prayers may be offered, concluding in a song which binds the group members together.

Suggested songs: 'Brother, sister, let me serve you' by Richard Gilliard; 'Bind us together, Lord'; 'All praise to our redeeming Lord' by Charles Wesley.

To close: A common pilgrim blessing involves pilgrims joining feet rather than hands. Ask the group to sit or stand so that their feet make contact with the feet either side of them. Invite the group to say the grace to one another. Such a blessing could be used each week if appropriate.

Group members may like to take their shells home with them to remind them of their ongoing pilgrimage. It will be important, however, for them to remember to bring them each week.

Session 2: Walking the story

Setting up the room

As in Week 1, allow time for people to settle if there has been a meal. Lay out the cloth, the candle, the ribbon and a few spare shells in case some have left theirs at home. Light the candle.

Opening worship and review of the journey (25 minutes)

Play some secular music that uses the imagery of life as a journey, e.g. 'Crossroads' by Don McClean, or 'The road is long' (He ain't heavy, he's my brother') by Sidney Russell and Robert Scott.

Ask people to talk with their neighbour about how they found the material this week. Have they managed to read Chapter 1? Did they try the meditations? How did they find the discipline of praying regularly? Have any insights come to them?

Invite people to place their shell on the cloth, placing it according to how they are feeling about this pilgrimage of faith. For example, near the ribbon if they feel they feel close to the path, or distant from it if they feel they are wandering without direction.

Ask the group, quietly, to pray for one another, wherever they are on the journey, finishing with the following prayer:

Lord Jesus Christ,
as we travel the road of our lives
there are many guides to show us the way
and many prophets proclaiming short cuts to happiness.
Travel with us, even along the byways that we take,
and help us to find, and rejoice in, the narrow way
that leads to life.
Amen.

Structured discussion A: To be a pilgrim (45 minutes)

Read Hebrews 11.13–16; 12.1–2

All of these died in faith without having received the promises, but from a distance they saw and greeted them. They confessed that they were strangers and pilgrims on the earth, for people who speak in this way make it clear that they are seeking a homeland. If they had been thinking of the land that they had left behind, they would have had opportunity to return. But as it is, they desire a better country, that is, a heavenly one. Therefore God is not ashamed to be called their God; indeed, he has prepared a city for them.

Therefore, since we are surrounded by so great a cloud of witnesses, let us also lay aside every weight and the sin that clings so closely, and let us run with perseverance the race that is set before us, looking to Jesus, the pioneer and perfecter of our faith, who for the sake of the joy that was set before him, endured the cross, disregarding its shame, and has taken his seat at the right hand of the throne of God.

In small groups ask people to discuss what this passage suggests to them about being a pilgrim (5 minutes).

Make some hymns and prayers available which mention pilgrims or pilgrimage. Ask the small groups to make a list of what makes a pilgrim (10 minutes).

Ask the small groups to brainstorm the differences between being a tourist and being a pilgrim (5 minutes).

Invite the whole group to discuss the question 'What are the characteristics of a Christian pilgrim?' (15 minutes). Invite the sharing of ideas from small group discussion and from any uses of the word they know, e.g. 'an ecumenical pilgrimage' or 'interfaith pilgrimage'. Draw in ideas from Chapter 1 to prompt and shape conversation as necessary:

- What role does discipline play in pilgrimage?
- What's the relationship between the outward journey and the inward journey for a pilgrim?
- How does the destination of a pilgrim shape the journey?
- Does the destination need to be fully known?

What else does seeing ourselves as pilgrims suggest about the ways in which Christians might approach life? (10 minutes).

- What role does discipline play in the Christian life?
- If the life of the Christian is the way of the cross, what are the qualities that such a life displays?

Structured discussion B: Living 'the good life' (45 minutes)

Read Matthew 5.2–12

Blessed are the poor in spirit, for theirs ix the kingdom of heaven.
Blessed are those who mourn, for they will be comforted.
Blessed are the meek, for they will inherit the earth.
Blessed are those who hunger and thirst for righteousness, for they will be filled.
Blessed are the merciful, for they will receive mercy.
Blessed are the pure in heart, for they will see God.

Blessed are the peacemakers, for they will be called children of God.

Blessed are those who are persecuted for righteousness' sake, for theirs is the kingdom of heaven.

Blessed are you when people revile you and persecute you and utter all kinds of evil against you falsely on my account. Rejoice and be glad, for your reward is great in heaven.

In small groups ask people to look at this passage and note down the values that shape its understanding of 'the good life' (5 minutes).

Make available some Sunday newspapers and ask the group to note down the values that shape these versions of 'the good life' (10 minutes).

Give people some personal space to think about how they spend their leisure time. (10 minutes)
- What TV programmes do they watch?
- What do they read?
- What music do they listen to?
- How do they spend their money?
- What is their attention directed towards?
- What messages are they getting about 'the good life'?

What stories of 'the good life' are we living out of as individuals, as a society, and as church communities? (10 minutes)
- Allow people to share personally if they wish;
- Invite people to speak about the lives of those they know instead.
- Draw out some of the material from the newspapers;
- and from the biblical passage.
- How do we tell which stories of 'the good life' are reinforcing a Christian way of life and which are drawing us away from it?

What can we do in practical terms to allow ourselves to be shaped more profoundly by the Christian story? (10 minutes)

Pause for reflection (10–15 minutes)

Ask the group to reflect quietly on their conversation:
- Do they feel any differently from when they arrived?
- Is there anything they want to remember from this evening?
- Is there anything they want to do differently as they leave this week?
- Are there any requests for prayer?

Give opportunity for those who wish to voice their personal reflections or to move their shell on the focal display.

Group review

Allow 5 minutes unless there are real issues to be addressed, in which case allow the time needed.

Closing prayers (5–10 minutes)

Include prayers of confession and assurance of forgiveness, and prayers of intercession as appropriate. Material may be drawn from some of the week's meditations.

To close: Ask the group to join their feet and pray the Lord's Prayer together.

Session 3: Pilgrim through this barren land

Setting up the room

As before. Allow time for people to settle if there has been a meal. Lay out the cloth, the candle, the ribbon and the shells. In addition, scatter on the cloth slips of paper on which are written phrases describing different frames of mind: e.g. confused, hopeful, exhausted, delighted, close to God, in pain, stuck in a rut, alone, despairing. A pen and slips of paper could be provided for people to write their own phrases.

Opening worship (5 minutes)

Play an excerpt from some music inspired by the natural world, e.g. from Haydn's *The Creation* or Vaughan Williams' *The Lark Ascending*.

Pray together:
> *Give us, O God, a vision of your glory*
> *that we may worship you in spirit and in truth,*
> *and offer the praise of glad and thankful hearts;*
> *through Christ our Lord.*
> *Amen.* (Methodist Worship Book, p.211)

Review of the journey this week (20 minutes)

Ask people to share something with their neighbour that has made an impact upon them during the week (either from the material or in any other part of their life).

Invite people to place their shell on the cloth where there is a word that matches their feeling about their journey this week. (The cloth should have already been prepared with short written phrases scattered along the route of the journey.)

Ask the group, quietly, to pray for one another, wherever they are on the journey.

Structured discussion A: Earth matters (45 minutes)

Read Psalm 19.1–4:

> *The heavens are telling the glory of God;*
> *and the firmament proclaims his handiwork.*
> *Day to day pours forth speech,*
> *and night to night declares knowledge.*
> *There is no speech, nor are there words;*

> *their voice is not heard;*
> *yet their voice goes out through all the earth,*
> *and their words to the end of the world.*

Ask people to spend some time on their own or in pairs thinking about the words of this psalm. Has it ever seemed to them that the natural world is praising God? (5 minutes)

Make available some poems/hymns which are about the natural world and ask people, in small groups, to note the ways in which these authors suggest that God relates to the natural world. Which do they find helpful? (10 minutes)

Ask the whole group to discuss how they think God relates to the natural world (15 minutes). What does their experience suggest? What kind of an ongoing relationship does God have with creation? Draw in ideas from Chapter 2 to prompt and shape conversation:
- Is God best seen as a remote initiator of the world?
- Can God only influence the inner thoughts of human beings and not the processes of nature?
- In what sense is God 'drawing all things together for good'?
- Does it make sense to think about the world as God's body?

Make the local newspapers available. Ask people to cut out the articles which indicate attitudes to the natural world. Are there any projects they want to support or want to oppose? (10 minutes)

Ask the group to consider how they think a sense of God's presence in the natural world should shape Christian attitudes towards it (5 minutes).

Structured discussion B: Becoming more human (45 minutes)
Read Genesis 2.7–9, 18–23a:

> *Then the LORD God formed [adam (a human)] from the dust of the ground [adamah], and breathed into his nostrils the breath of life; and [adam] became a living being. And the LORD God planted a garden in Eden, in the east; and there he put adam, whom he had formed. Out of the ground the Lord God made to grow every tree that is pleasant to the sight and good for food, the tree of life also in the midst of the garden, and the tree of the knowledge of good and evil. Then the LORD God said, 'It is not good that [adam] should be alone; I will make him a helper as his partner.' So out of the ground the LORD God formed every animal of the field and every bird of the air, and brought to [adam] to see what he would call them; and whatever [adam] called every living creature, that was its name. [Adam] gave names to all cattle, and to the birds of the air, and to every animal of*

148

the field; but for [adam] there was not found a helper as his partner. So the LORD God caused a deep sleep to fall upon [adam], and he slept; then he took one of his ribs and closed up its place with flesh. And the rib that the LORD God had taken from [adam] he made into a woman and brought her to [adam]. Then [adam] said, 'This at last is bone of my bones and flesh of my flesh.'

Ask people to work in small groups to make a list of what they think makes us human (5 minutes).

Ask the groups to look at the biblical passage. What is implied there about being human? (5 minutes)

Invite people to think about the things they do that they find most humanizing (5 minutes) and talk to their neighbour about how these activities make them feel (5 minutes).

Ask the whole group the question 'What is life in all its fullness?' (15 minutes). Draw on people's experience, the biblical passage and Chapter 2 to shape the discussion:
- What does their experience of 'feeling human' suggest about the nature of fullness of life?
- What has fullness of life to do with being in touch with our creatureliness?
- What does it mean to worship with our being?

What aspects of the Christian life would the group recommend as being of value to those seeking to become more fully human? (10 minutes)
- Personal prayer?
- Meditation?
- Worship services?
- Belonging to a community?
- A sense of vision/purpose?
- Other things?

Pause for reflection (10–15 minutes)

Ask the group to reflect quietly on their conversation:
- Do they feel any differently from when they arrived?
- Is there anything they want to remember from this evening?
- Is there anything they want to do differently as they leave this week?
- Are there any requests for prayer?

Give opportunity for those who wish to voice their personal reflections, or to move their shell, or add a word to the focal display.

Group review

Allow 5 minutes unless there are real issues to be addressed, in which case allow the time needed. Remind people that next week they are invited to bring with them a picture of Christ.

Closing prayers (5 minutes)

Include prayers of confession and assurance of forgiveness, and prayers of intercession as appropriate.

Blessing

Ask the group to join their feet and say together this traditional Celtic blessing which is rooted in the natural world:

May the road rise to meet you;
may the wind be always at your back;
may the sun shine warmly on your face;
and the rain fall softly on your fields;
and, until we meet again, may God hold you
in the hollow of his hand.
Amen.

Session 4: Christ the pilgrim

Setting up the room

As before, lay out the cloth, the candle, the ribbon and the shells. Place some small mirrors on the cloth. Mirror tiles can be bought quite cheaply if necessary. In addition, place on the cloth several pictures or statues of Jesus. Old Christmas cards can be a good source of such images.

Opening worship and review of the journey this week (25 minutes)

Read 1 John 1.1: *We declare to you what was from the beginning, what we have heard, what we have seen with our eyes, what we have looked at and touched with our hands – the Word of Life – this is our theme.* (New Jerusalem Bible)

Sing or play a recording of a hymn to Christ, such as 'Shine, Jesus, shine' by Graham Kendrick or 'Love divine, all loves excelling' by Charles Wesley.

Ask people to share with their neighbour the image of Christ they have brought. If anybody has forgotten, they could choose an image from the cloth (10 minutes).

Invite everyone to pick up a mirror and place it next to their image of Christ. Invite people to look into the mirror and think about their journey this week (5 minutes).

As people hold their mirror and their picture of Jesus side by side, lead this prayer:

> *Christ, our fellow pilgrim,*
> *you walk with us on the way,*
> *even when we are blind to your presence.*
> *Hidden companion, you are closer to us*
> *than we are to ourselves.*
> *Draw us deeper into our own reality*
> *that we may meet you face to face.*
> *Amen.*

Invite the group to place their mirrors and images of Christ on the cloth, together with their shells.

Structured discussion A: The image of Christ

Read: Colossians 1.15-19:

> *He is the image of the invisible God, the first-born of all creation; for in him all things in heaven and on earth were created, things visible and invisible, whether thrones or dominions or rulers or powers – all things have been created through him and for him. He*

151

himself is before all things, and in him all things hold together. He is the head of the body, the church; he is the beginning, the firstborn from the dead, so that he might come to have first place in everything. For in him all the fullness of God was pleased to dwell.

In small groups ask people to look at this passage and make a list of all the images used to express who Christ is. Which do the group find helpful in connecting them with God and which distance them? (5 minutes)

In small groups, ask people to think about a story or saying of Jesus that helps them know that Christ is for them. Ask them to tell each other the story and to draw out the features that move them (15 minutes).

In the whole group, ask people how they came to identify with Christ. Draw in their stories and the images they brought. Draw in ideas from Chapter 3 (15 minutes):
- What has helped them – stories, pictures, poems, experiences?
- How prominent is Jesus in their spirituality, compared with God the Father or the Holy Spirit, or the Trinity as a whole?
- How do people make sense of the belief that Christ relates to the whole human race? What images or pictures are helpful there?
- How did they come to realize that they personally are related to God in Christ?

Ask the group how can we make such experiences available to those who do not come to church? (10 minutes)

Looking at what has helped those in this group to identify with Christ, what might help an unchurched generation?
- Can art be a tool? Can this be public art – used outside buildings?
- Is film useful?
- Is Jesus the place to start?

Structured discussion B: Reality church

Read James 5.13–16a:

Are any among you suffering? They should pray. Are any cheerful? They should sing songs of praise. Are any among you sick? They should call for the elders of the church and have them pray over them, anointing them with oil in the name of the Lord. The prayer of faith will save the sick, and the Lord will raise them up; and anyone who has committed sins will be forgiven. Therefore confess your sins to one another, so that you may be healed.

In small groups invite people to look at this passage and think about the kind of community it describes (5 minutes).

Have you ever been part of a church or group in which you are able to let others in on your journey: confessing your sins and receiving forgiveness or asking for prayer? (10 minutes)

In the whole group, discuss what contributes to, or prevents, a church community being able to bear one another's burdens and share one another's journeys. Draw on people's experience. Draw also on Chapter 3 to shape the conversation as necessary (15 minutes):
- What prevents people sharing more of themselves in churches?
- Can people share themselves with Christ if not with others?
- What is the importance of being real – of 'making a journey into our own reality'?
- What/who helps them to be real with themselves and with God?
- What about the dynamics of this group?

If Christ is about helping us to be real, what has Christianity to offer the wider culture? Refer the group to the picture of the naked pilgrim (15 minutes).
- Encourage the group to think about reality TV.
- Why is it popular?
- Is it about being real or exposure?
- What is the difference?
- How can we encourage more 'being real' in our families and workplaces and local communities?
- How much of this is to do with creating safe enough communities in which people can be vulnerable?
- How is Christ relevant to this?

Pause for reflection (10–15 minutes)
Suggest the group pick up their mirrors and images of Christ again.

Ask them to reflect quietly on their conversation:
- Do they feel any differently from when they arrived?
- Is there anything they want to remember from this evening?
- Is there anything they want to do differently as they leave this week?
- Are there any requests for prayer?

Ask the group to pray quietly for one another.

Group review

Allow 5 minutes unless there are real issues to be addressed, in which case allow the time needed.

Closing prayers (5 minutes)

To close ask the group to join their feet and to pray together:

Christ be with me, Christ within me,
Christ behind me, Christ before me,
Christ beside me, Christ to win me,
Christ to comfort and restore me.
Christ beneath me, Christ above me,
Christ in quiet, Christ in danger,
Christ in hearts of all that love me,
Christ in mouth of friend and stranger.

Session 5: Strangers and pilgrims

Setting up the room

As before, lay out the cloth, the candle, the ribbon and the shells. Provide a small loaf of bread and a cup of water which can be shared in the closing worship. There also need to be slips of paper and pens available as well as national newspapers if you are choosing Option A.

Opening worship and review of the journey this week (25 minutes)

Light the candle.

Sing or read together, 'Guide me, O thou great redeemer', by William Williams or a version of Psalm 23 like 'The King of love my Shepherd is' by Henry Baker.

Read 1 Kings 19.4–8:

> *[Elijah] went a day's journey into the wilderness, and came and sat down under a solitary broom tree. He asked that he might die: 'It is enough; now O LORD, take away my life, for I am no better than my ancestors.' Then he lay down under the broom tree and fell asleep. Suddenly an angel touched him and said to him, 'Get up and eat.' He looked, and there at his head was a cake baked on hot stones, and a jar of water. He ate and drank, and lay down again. The angel of the LORD came to him a second time and said, 'Get up and eat, otherwise the journey will be too much for you.' He got up, and ate and drank; then hewent on in the strength of that food forty days and forty nights to Horeb the mount of God.*

Invite people to think of times when they have felt exhausted and depleted like Elijah. Who have been their angels providing food and touch and strength for the journey? (5 minutes)

Invite people to share a story of being met and fed by someone when they were in need (10 minutes).

Invite the group to write the names of their 'angels' on a piece of paper and place it with their shell somewhere along the ribbon.

> *Lord, our God,*
> *the source of our life and the sustainer of our faith,*
> *we thank you for those who have met us and fed us along life's way.*
> *We remember those who have held us when we were in despair;*
> *those whose practical care has put body and soul back together*
> *when we were exhausted;*
> *and those who have fed us with wisdom*

when we did not know which way to turn.
We recall their faces and thank you for the life and faith
they have nurtured in us as angels of your presence.
Amen.

Structured discussion A: Guests at the feast (45 minutes)

Read Hebrews 13.1–3, 5–6:

> *Let mutual love continue. Do not neglect to show hospitality to strangers, for by doing that some have entertained angels without knowing it. Remember those who are in prison, as though you were in prison with them; those who are being tortured, as though yourselves were being tortured. Keep your lives free from the love of money, and be content with what you have; for he has said, 'I will never leave you or forsake you.' So we can say with confidence,*
> > *'The Lord is my helper;*
> > *I will not be afraid.*
> > *What can anyone do to me?'*

Ask the small groups to look at the national newspapers. What attitudes towards strangers are evidenced here? What is behind these attitudes? (10 minutes)

Ask the small groups to look at the passage from Hebrews. What governs attitudes to strangers here? Where does the courage to hold these attitudes come from? How do these compare with our attitudes to prisoners and asylum seekers and to those tortured or radically different from us? (10 minutes)

In the whole group, discuss the question 'What governs human attitudes towards strangers?' (15 minutes)
- Encourage people to draw on their own feelings as well as newspaper stories.
- Who do we find most threatening? (Encourage people to be real – those with mental illness? 'Terrorists'? 'Hoodies'? Gay people?)
- Which of these fears are founded?
- What does the Bible have to say about these attitudes? (Chapter 4 discusses the visit to Abraham; instructions to the Israelites to remember that they were strangers in Egypt; the parable of the sheep and the goats.)

In the whole group, discuss the value of the concept of hospitality for today's world (10 minutes):
What would it mean, in practical terms, to live this way of life
- in our homes and schools?
- in local and national politics?
- as individuals and as church communities?

Structured discussion B: The Church as guest (45 minutes)

Read Luke 10.1–11:

> *After this the Lord appointed seventy others and sent them on ahead of him in pairs to every town and place where he himself intended to go. He said to them, 'The harvest is plentiful but the labourers are few; therefore ask the Lord of the harvest to send out labourers into his harvest. Go on your way. See, I am sending you out like lambs into the midst of wolves. Carry no purse, no bag, no sandals; and greet no one on the road. Whatever house you enter, first say, "Peace to this house!" And if anyone is there who shares in peace, your peace will rest on that person; but if not, it will return to you. Remain in the same house, eating and drinking whatever they provide, for the labourer deserves to be paid. Do not move about from house to house. Whenever you enter a town and its people welcome you, eat what is set before you; cure the sick who are there, and say to them, "The kingdom of God has come near to you." But whenever you enter a town and they do not welcome you, go out into its streets and say, "Even the dust of your town that clings to our feet, we wipe off in protest against you. Yet know this: the kingdom of God has come near."'*

In small groups, ask people to make a list of the instructions to the disciples. Which do they find striking? (5 minutes)

For many years, in the West, the Church has had power and influence in society and has seen itself as the benevolent host. Here the disciples are sent out as guests into the homes of strangers. Ask the group to think of times when they have been guests in the houses of strangers (10 minutes):

- What did it feel like? Were they made welcome?
- From where did they draw strength?
- Were they there as private individuals or as ambassadors of someone else?
- Did this make a difference?
- Ask the groups to draw on the passage and on their own experience to think about the virtues that are needed to be a gracious guest.

In the whole group, ask people to reflect on how many of the instructions given to the disciples in this passage are relevant to the Church in western society today (15 minutes):

- Are we called to be guests rather than hosts in today's world?
- What are the advantages and disadvantages of proclaiming the kingdom as guests and not hosts?
- Are we being sent out of church buildings?
- What should we take with us?
- To what kind of strange places is God calling us?

Finally, ask the group to consider what new skills, support and resources they need in order to answer the call to go out like lambs amid wolves!

Pause for reflection (10–15 minutes)

Ask them to reflect quietly on their conversation:
- How have you found the conversation?
- Is there anything you want to remember and take away?
- Is there any action you want to take as a result of this meeting?
- Do you have any requests for prayer?

Option A: Invite people to place newspaper clippings about strangers on the cloth.

Option B: Invite people to write the names of those groups or strange places to which they believe the Church today is being called to go.

Invite the group to pray quietly in response to those mentioned and requests made.

Group review

Allow 5 minutes unless there are real issues to be addressed, in which case allow the time needed.

Closing prayers (5 minutes)

Isaiah 55.1a: *Ho, everyone who thirsts, come to the waters;*
and you that have no money, come, buy and eat!

The bread and the water are passed around the circle for people to eat and drink.

To close ask the group to join their feet and to pray together:

Gracious God,
you have fed us with the bread of heaven and the water of life.
Send us out in the power of your Spirit
as guests of the world and servants of your kingdom.
Amen.

Session 6: Coming home

Setting up the room

As before, lay out the cloth, the candle, the ribbon and the shells. Place some of the objects from previous weeks around the cloth to remind people of the journey they have taken and make a basket of small pebbles available – enough for each person to have four or five.

Opening worship and review of the journey this week (5 minutes)

Light the candle.

Leader: I was glad when they said to me,
'Let us go to the house of the LORD!'
All: **Our feet are standing
within your gates, O Jerusalem.**   (Psalm 122.1-2)

Leader: Those who trust in the Lord are like Mount Zion
which cannot be moved, but abides forever.
All: **As the mountains surround Jerusalem,
So the LORD surrounds his people,
from this time on and for evermore.**   (Psalm 125.1-2)

Leader: Unless the LORD builds the house,
those who build it labour in vain.
All: **Unless the LORD guards the city,
the guard keeps watch in vain.**   (Psalm 127.1)

Leader: It is in vain that you rise up early and go late to rest,
eating the bread of anxious toil;
for he gives sleep to his beloved.   (Psalm 127.2)

O taste and see that the LORD is good:
All: **happy are those who take refuge in him.**   (Psalm 34.8)

Sing or play a song such as, 'I will enter his gates with thanksgiving in my heart' by Gwen R. Shaw, or 'We have come into his house to worship him' by Bruce Ballinger, or a setting of Psalm 95.

Review of the journey so far (20 minutes)

Invite people to trace in their mind the journey they have taken during this course, using the visual cues on the cloth. What have been the challenging points? Where have they been fed? Where were the places of encounter? Invite people to place small pebbles on the cloth to represent moments of significance along the way.

Invite people to share some of thier thoughts with their neighbour.

When they are ready, invite the group to place their shells as near to the candle as they feel is appropriate as this is almost the end of the journey.

Structured discussion A: Heaven is our home (45 minutes)

Read 2 Corinthians 5.1–10:

> For we know that if the earthly tent we live in is destroyed, we have a building from God, a house not made with human hands, eternal in the heavens. For in this tent we groan, longing to be clothed with our heavenly dwelling – if indeed, when we have taken it off, we will not be found naked. For while we are still in this tent, we groan under our burden, because we wish not to be unclothed but to be further clothed, so that what is mortal may be swallowed up by life. He who has prepared us for this very thing is God, who has given us the Spirit as a guarantee. So we are always confident; even though we know that while we are at home in the body, we are away from the Lord – for we walk by faith, not by sight. Yes, we do have confidence, and we would rather be away from the body and at home with the Lord. So whether we are at home or away, we make it our aim to please him. For all of us must appear before the judgement seat of Christ, so that each may receive recompense for what has been done in the body, whether good or evil.

Ask people to think of a time when they have been away – perhaps in hospital or on a difficult journey – and then come home. What did it feel like to come home? Tell the story to a neighbour (10 minutes).

The Bible often speaks about heaven as a house or home. In small groups, note down how heaven is described in this passage (5 minutes).
- Provide the small groups with some copies of the funeral liturgies, for example, from *The Methodist Worship Book* or from *Common Worship*. Ask them to note the images in the prayers and biblical passages. What do they find helpful?

As a whole group, ask people to discuss what they think heaven is like. Refer them to the biblical passage and to the ideas in Chapter 5 (15 minutes).
- Is it like a homecoming – in what ways?
- What role does judgement play?
- Is it good news for us that Christ is our judge?
- What do Christians mean by proclaiming the resurrection of the body?
- How does our bodily life connect with our 'bodily' life after death?

How are we to live as those who are prepared for death? (15 minutes)
- Is death much discussed in homes and families?
- Is life beyond death talked about in church?
- What helps us to acknowledge our mortality in a healthy way?

Structured discussion B: Gateways to heaven (45 minutes)

Read John 20.11–16, 19–23:

But Mary stood weeping outside the tomb. As she wept, she bent over to look into the tomb; and she saw two angels in white, sitting where the body of Jesus had been lying, one at the head and the other at the feet. They said to her, 'Woman, why are you weeping?' She said to them, 'They have taken away my Lord, and I do not know where they have laid him.' When she had said this, she turned around and saw Jesus standing there, but she did not know that it was Jesus. Jesus said to her, 'Woman, why are weeping? For whom are you looking?' Supposing him to be the gardener, she said to him, 'Sir, if you have carried him away, tell me where you have laid him, and I will take him away.' Jesus said to her, 'Mary!' She turned and said to him in Hebrew, 'Rabbouni!' (which means Teacher).

When it was evening on that day, the first day of the week, and the doors of the house where the disciples had met were locked for fear of the Jews, Jesus came and stood among them and said, 'Peace be with you.' After he said this, he showed them his hands and his side. Then the disciples rejoiced when they saw the Lord. Jesus said to them again, 'Peace be with you. As the Father has sent me, so I send you.' When he had said this, he breathed on them and said to them, 'Receive the Holy Spirit. If you forgive the sins of any, they are forgiven them; if you retain the sins of any, they are retained.'

Ask people to think of any places or people they would name as holy. Invite them to describe these places to one another in small groups (10 minutes).

Invite the small groups to look at this biblical passage. Can the garden tomb be described as a holy place? Might the disciples, in any sense, be described as holy people? (5 minutes)

Working with the whole group, ask people to discuss the idea of holy place. Encourage people to reflect on their own experience as well as the ideas in Chapter 5 (15 minutes).
- What makes a place holy?
- Can a tomb be a holy place?
- Is a holy place a place where people have met God before? Does that make it likely that God will be encountered there again?
- Has the growth of shrines at the sides of the road – or the desire of people to enter churches to light candles at times of disaster – got anything to do with holy place?

- If churches are intended to be houses for meeting with God, how can we help people to do that? (Use of space; use of silence; use of visual imagery, etc.?)

Ask the whole group to think about the idea of holy people (15 minutes):
- What makes a person holy?
- Are those who have received the Holy Spirit meeting places with God?
- Who, among the Christian community, are called to be holy in this way? (Only the apostles, those officially named as saints, clergy or all Christians?)
- What helps us to be open to the Holy Spirit so that others might meet God in us?

Pause for reflection and group review (15 minutes)

At the end of any group's life, it is important for its members to be able to acknowledge the ending and make plans for the future – both as a group and as individuals. Make sure that you allow people to reflect personally on the following:
- on the whole pilgrimage they have made;
- noting any insights they will take away;
- noting any changes they want to make in the way they live.

Also, help the group to think about its common life:
- Has the group performed an important role for people – if so, what?
- Should the group continue or come to a natural end?
- What would its aims be if it carried on?
- Might others benefit from the material used in a different context e.g. another group; a worship service?
- Would any members of the group be interested in leading such a group or service?

When people have had a chance to share their thoughts, invite them to take up their shells. The journey does not end here – for each one – it continues.

Closing prayers (5 minutes)

To close ask the group to join their feet and say together:

> *Sisters and brothers,*
> *at this time of parting we are confident that God knows us and is with us.*
> *As we look back over our journey together*
> *we offer our thanks for your presence with us in time of grief and of joy;*
> *we receive your forgiveness for moments of impatience and misunderstanding;*
> *we pray for one another as we journey from this place;*
> *and we ask for your blessing as we seek to follow Jesus Christ to our life's end,*
> *Amen.*

A song may be sung, such as 'This, this is the God we adore' by Joseph Hart; or 'O Jesus, I have promised', by John Ernest Bode.

Leader: The peace of the Lord be always with you:
All: **and also with you.**

The Peace is shared as people prepare to leave.

Suggestions for Further Reading

On pilgrimage

C. Bartholomew and F. Hughes (eds.), *Explorations in a Christian Theology of Pilgrimage*, Sheffield: Aldershot, 2004.

Jane Leach, 'Camino de Santiago: The Value and Significance of Pilgrimage in the Twenty-first Century', *Epworth Review* 33:1 (2006), pp. 31–39.

Martin Robinson, *Sacred Places, Pilgrim Paths: An anthology of pilgrimage*, London, Fount: Marshall Pickering, 1997.

On the natural world and ecology

Mary Grey, *Beyond the Dark Night: A way forward for the Church?*, London, Cassell 1997.

Sallie McFague, *The Body of God: An Ecological Theology*, Minneapolis, Fortress 1993.

On Christology

Julie Hopkins, *Towards a Feminist Christology: Jesus of Nazareth, European Women and the Christological Crisis*, Kampen, Kok Pharos, 1994.

Clive Marsh, *Christ in Practice: A Christology of Everyday Life*, London, Darton Longman and Todd, 2006

On hospitality in a plural world

J.R. Middleton and B.J. Walsh, *Truth Is Stranger than it Used to Be: Biblical Faith in a Postmodern Age*, London, SPCK, 1995.

Miroslav Volf, *Exclusion and Embrace: theological exploration of identity, otherness and reconciliation*, Nashville, Abingdon, 1996.

Zygmunt Bauman, *Postmodern Ethics*, Oxford, Blackwell, 1993.

On holy place and the role of saints

John Inge, *A Christian Theology of Place*, Aldershot, Ashgate, 2003.

Philip Sheldrake, *Spaces for the Sacred: Place, memory and identity*, London, SCM Press, 1981.

Peter Brown, *The Cult of The Saints: its rise and function in Latin Christianity*, Chicago, University of Chicago,1981.

Prayers, poems and meditations for pilgrims

Francis Dewar, *Invitations: God's calling for everyone*, London, SPCK, 1996.

Robert Ferré, *Praying the Chartres Labyrinth: A pilgrim's guidebook*, Derby, Pilgrim Press, 2006.

Henri J. Nouwen, *Bread for the Journey: Reflections for every day of the year*, London, Darton, Longman and Todd, 1996.
Rainer Maria Rilke, *The Book of Hours: Love poems to God*, trans. Anita Burrows and Joanna Macy, New York, Riverhead Books, 1996.
Helen Raphael Sands, *Walking the Healing Labyrinth*, London, Gala Books, 2005.
Joby Tallbot, *The Path of Miracles*, recorded by Tenebrae with Signum Records, 2006.
Rowan Williams, *Ponder these things: Praying with icons of the Virgin*, Norwich, Canterbury Press, 2002.

For information about walking the Camino de Santiago contact The Confraternity of St James: www.csj.org.uk

Acknowledgements

Chapter 1

Annunciation from San Juan de Ortega, permission sought.

Chapter 3

Frieze of Christ and the disciples on the road to Emmaus and Frieze of Doubting Thomas © Abadia de Sto. Domingo de Silos, used with permission.

Chapter 5

Cathedral of Santiago de Compostela, permission sought.